MINI-CFO
ADVENTURES
A Kid's Journey to
Chief Financial Officer Wisdom

Dr. Joy Chacko

Skillful Adventures™ Series

Mini-CFO Adventures: A Kid's Journey to Chief Financial Officer Wisdom

Originally published in 2025 by Joy Chacko, PhD

Part of the Skillful Adventures™ Series

ISBN: 979-8-9934027-6-5

(Economy Edition – Black & White Interior)

Publisher: Skillful Adventures Press

SkillfulAdventures.com

Mini-CFO Adventures transforms financial wisdom into storytelling magic—delivered with unforgettable clarity and delight for young readers.

Through imaginative journeys, real-world concepts, and powerful character lessons, children learn to think strategically, make confident decisions, and understand how money, business, and leadership work. It's a joyful pathway to lifelong financial intelligence—shaping tomorrow's thinkers, doers, and leaders.

✸ Skillful Adventures™ Series ✸

Stories Kids Love. Skills They Keep for Life.

✸ Time Management Adventures — Master time with fun strategies and daily success habits.

✸ Project Management Adventures — Turn ideas into projects and projects into success!

✸ Mini-CFO Adventures — Discover how money works and how to grow it wisely.

✸ Leadership Adventures — Build confidence, teamwork, and a vision that inspires.

And more Skillful Adventures™ are on the way!

✸ Visit SkillfulAdventures.com

Table of Contents

Section 1:

The Foundations of Financial Thinking

Theme: *From curiosity to clarity — helping children understand how money works and why financial intelligence matters. This section builds awareness around earning, learning, and the power of taking action.*

Meet the Heroes

Before this adventure begins, let's meet our friends from Prosperity Hollow:

- **Timmy the Tortoise:** Calm and steady, Timmy always takes his time to think before he acts.

- **Bella the Bunny:** Quick and full of energy, Bella hops from one activity to another — sometimes a bit too fast!

- **Max the Monkey:** Clever and curious, Max loves solving problems and finding fun new ideas.

- **Lily the Ladybug:** Organized and thoughtful, Lily enjoys making lists and helping her friends stay on track.

And guiding them all is **Professor FinanceWise** (many also call him **Professor Timeless Wisdom**) — the wise owl known across Prosperity Hollow by many names. In this adventure, he teaches how smart decisions, clear thinking, and good financial habits shape a bright future.

Chapter 1

Welcome to Prosperity Hollow – The Mini-CFO Journey Begins

The Magical Town of Prosperity Hollow

O nce upon a time, deep within the enchanted forest of Clocksville, where towering trees whispered secrets of old and crystal-clear rivers sparkled under the sun, there lay a vibrant town known as *Prosperity Hollow.*

Nestled at the heart of the forest, Prosperity Hollow was no ordinary town—it was a place where ideas turned into gold, where merchants bartered with a twinkle in their eye, and where the young and old alike learned the art of wealth.

On this particular day, the town square was alive with bakers selling warm pastries, merchants showcasing handcrafted goods, and young apprentices eagerly learning trades from wise elders. The air buzzed with excitement as traders from distant lands arrived with exotic goods—silken fabrics from the East, fragrant spices from the South, and shimmering gemstones from the mountain caves.

The Hall of Wisdom – A Place of Great Learning

At the heart of the town square stood a grand old building—the Hall of Wisdom. It wasn't just a place of learning; it was where the secrets of money, business, and prosperity were passed down through generations. Here, townspeople learned how to grow their wealth, manage resources, and build businesses that could last a lifetime.

And today, four curious friends—Timmy the Tortoise, Bella the Bunny, Max the Monkey, and Lily the Ladybug—had come to the Hall of Wisdom, eager to unlock its greatest secrets. They had heard whispers of a powerful truth—one that could help them understand how money worked, how businesses grew, and how they could shape their own future.

As they stepped inside, the soft glow of lanterns illuminated endless scrolls, golden coins stacked in careful piles, and intricate maps showing trade routes across the land. And there, perched high on his majestic wooden stand, adjusting his tiny pocket watch, was none other than Professor Timeless Wisdom, the wise old owl.

"Ah, my young students," the Professor hooted warmly, "you've come at just the right time. Today, I shall teach you one of the most important lessons of all—how to make money work for you instead of working only for money."

The four friends leaned in closer, their eyes wide with anticipation.

A Mysterious Conversation in the Market

But before the Professor could continue, they overheard a conversation near the market stalls. A merchant and a baker were discussing numbers.

"You must not be keeping track of your accounts properly!" the merchant said.

"You must have forgotten the basic accounting equation!"

The four friends exchanged puzzled glances.

"What does he mean by 'accounting equation'?" Bella whispered.

The Professor chuckled. "Ah, my young friends, before you can make money work for you, you must first understand how money moves. And to do that, you need to learn the first rule of business—the Accounting Equation."

He lifted his wing and scribbled something in the air with his feathered tip:

Assets = Liabilities + Equity

The friends gasped. "What does that mean?" Max asked eagerly.

The Professor's eyes twinkled. "That, my curious young learners, is the first step toward financial wisdom. But let's take it one step at a time. Are you ready for the challenge?"

The four friends nodded eagerly. Their adventure was just beginning…

Reflection Time — What We Learned

As the day quiets in Prosperity Hollow, Professor FinanceWise offers one final reminder:

"Every choice you make with clarity and purpose becomes a building block of your future."

Key Takeaway for Kids

Smart earning, thoughtful saving, wise spending, and careful risk-taking help you grow into a confident, responsible leader.

Final Inspiration

"Your future begins with the decisions you make today. Choose wisely, grow boldly."

Chapter 2

Execution Wins: How Taking Action Creates Wealth

W hat makes the difference between people who talk about success and those who actually create it? This story follows two individuals—one highly educated, the other self-driven—and the very different results their choices produced. It's a lesson in action, initiative, and execution.

Far beyond the magical forests of Clocksville, where the wisdom of wealth was cherished, lay a bustling modern city where two individuals sat quietly on a bench—one a high school dropout struggling for work, the other an MBA graduate recently out of a job.

The Dropout sighed. "I've been to so many interviews today, but no one will hire me."

The MBA nodded. "I understand how you feel. I worked for a big company, but I was fired because I wouldn't change the numbers to make my boss look good. Now, I can't find a new job either."

The Dropout looked surprised. "But you have a degree! You should have no trouble finding work."

The MBA shook his head. "Degrees are important, but I wish I had learned skills that I could use in any situation—like how to start a business."

The Dropout's eyes widened. "So, what should I do?"

The MBA thought for a moment. "Start something small. Something that people need every day. You don't need a lot of money—just determination."

The Dropout asked, "Then why haven't you started a business?"

The MBA hesitated. "I've thought about it, but I keep waiting for the perfect idea."

The Dropout smiled. "Well, I don't have time to wait."

Taking Action vs. Waiting for the Perfect Moment

The Dropout borrowed **$100** from a friend and bought some lawn care equipment. He asked a neighbor if he could mow their lawn for a small fee. Soon, he had **10 clients**. By six months, he had **30 clients**. Within a year, he had over **200 clients** and even **hired a bookkeeper** to manage his growing business.

Two years later, he sat on the same bench in the shopping mall. This time, he wasn't looking for a job—he was looking for someone to **help grow his company**.

That's when he saw the MBA again.

"You must have started a great business by now," the Dropout said.

The MBA sighed. "No... I've been looking for a job, but I haven't found the right one."

The Dropout smiled. "Well, I took your advice. I started a lawn care business. Now, I have **employees, a truck, and a growing company.**"

The MBA was amazed. "That's incredible!"

"Actually," the Dropout said, "I need someone who understands **business strategy, hiring, and marketing.** You know those things, right?"

The MBA nodded.

"Then come work for me! Be my **CFO** and help me expand."

And so, the MBA, who once thought only about jobs, joined the business world and helped **build one of the largest lawn care companies in the country**.

Reflection

Education opens doors, but financial intelligence and decisive action create opportunities. Success comes to those who start with what they have, take small steps, and learn along the way. No matter your background, **execution—taking action, not waiting or staying idle—is the strongest path to growth.**

Final Inspiration

"Small steps create big futures—start today."

EFFORT + VALUE = EARNING

= Effort
= Value
= Earning

$1 Per Glass

Chapter 3

The Mini-CFO's Strategic Earning Mindset

The friends gathered under their favorite mango tree on the edge of Prosperity Hollow. Timmy the Tortoise polished his coin jar. Bella the Bunny sketched in her notebook. Max the Monkey hung upside down from a branch, flipping through a flyer: "Pet Walking – $5/hour." Lily the Ladybug buzzed nearby, balancing her tiny chalkboard.

Professor FinanceWise arrived with his usual flair—briefcase in hand, glasses slightly tilted.

"Ah! A perfect morning to talk about **Earning**!" he declared. "Let's unlock one of the greatest superpowers of the Mini-CFO!"

What Is Earning?

Professor FinanceWise flipped open Bella's sketchpad and drew a simple chart:

EFFORT + VALUE = EARNING

"Earning," he explained, "is when you do something valuable and others give you something in return. It could be money. It could be praise. It could be learning. Even a thank-you."

Timmy raised a slow hand. "So… when I help Granny Tortoise carry groceries, is that earning?"

"If it creates value for her—and she rewards you in some way—then yes!" said Professor FinanceWise.

Max scratched his head. "Even if she just gives me her famous mango jam?"

"Especially then," the Professor smiled.

Starting Small Is Smart

Bella pulled out her Bright Ideas List:

- Chores at home
- Walking pets
- Lemonade stand
- Selling crafts online

- Tutoring
- Starting a YouTube or art channel
- Offering simple services as a freelancer (like helping with art, writing, or small jobs)

"These are all real and awesome ways to earn," Bella said. "They helped me buy my art supplies last year!"

"Indeed," nodded Professor FinanceWise. "Every earning journey begins somewhere. But today, let's think bigger—let's talk about *Earnings Plus*."

Introducing: Earnings Plus

Professor FinanceWise grinned and picked up the chalk.

"Earnings Plus," he wrote on the big chalkboard, "means earning that grows your future—every step teaches, builds skills, and opens new doors."

Lily's eyes lit up. She copied the phrase, then added bold, colorful letters on her own board:

Earnings Plus = Earning That Grows Your Future

"I want my gig to be an Earnings Plus gig!" she declared.

Professor FinanceWise nodded. "Great thinking, Lily! Earnings Plus is not just about the money you make—it's about how each opportunity helps you learn, build, and launch your next big step."

He turned to the friends. "Here are the Mini-CFO's Strategic Earning Habits:"

- "Pick gigs that help you grow future skills," he explained. "Look for work that sharpens your creativity, tech skills, people skills, or leadership."

- "Choose roles that can give you more than money—like mentorship, learning, or new connections."

- "And always see every role, task, or gig as a stepping stone. Ask yourself, 'What can this lead to next?'"

Bella raised her hand. "So even if I start with a lemonade stand, I should think about what I'm learning for my next steps?"

"Exactly!" said Professor FinanceWise. "Earnings Plus makes every gig part of your bigger, future journey."

Real Story: The Housekeeper Who Became a Doctor

Professor FinanceWise opened his scrapbook, revealing the legend of an Earnings Plus Hero.

Inside was the story of a high school girl who found a part-time job as a hospital housekeeper.

"Not very glamorous," said Max.

Professor FinanceWise nodded. "No, but very smart! She wasn't just earning a paycheck — she was also building long-term benefits, like Social Security credits and savings accounts that help her money grow over time. Most teens don't really realize how these benefits work, or that they can start using them even at a young age!"

Professor FinanceWise paused. "But she wanted to do even more for her patients and be part of the hospital's bigger mission. Her heart and mind were set on making lasting changes in patient care, so she worked hard to learn and grow."

"What happened next?" asked Lily, wide-eyed.

"Well," said Professor FinanceWise, "she was promoted to anesthesia technician while attending community college—some of her tuition was paid by the hospital. Next, she entered nursing school, fully supported and financially aided by her employer. Over time, as an RN, she kept learning, saving, and investing—building a strong foundation for her future career and financial well-being."

Professor FinanceWise continued, "Her extraordinary work and dedication earned her strong recommendations from her team. When she decided to attend medical school, she chose to stay within the same hospital system. While hospitals do not usually pay full medical school tuition, she received scholarships, financial aid, and support through grants aligned with the hospital's mission to train future doctors. After graduating from medical school, she returned to the hospital as a resident doctor, continuing her training—a house doctor—within the same system."

Bella gasped, "And get this—she became a doctor at the same hospital she once cleaned!"

Professor FinanceWise beamed. "The hospital team was thrilled to welcome her back—not just because she was smart, but because she had built a reputation for discipline, kindness, and teamwork. She grew both her career—and her financial future—by thinking strategically, planning ahead, and acting on opportunities others overlooked."

He tapped the chalkboard, where the steps were written:

- Earn Early
- Grow Skills
- Build a Network
- Think Long-Term
- Do your research and take real action—seek out opportunities in your area of interest that help you earn, learn, and grow while building your path to financial confidence. Don't wait or get lazy!

"Her story is a Mini-CFO masterclass," said Professor FinanceWise. "Think big, make life meaningful, and build both wealth and wisdom. Always ask: Where can this role, this skill, or this connection lead me?"

Your Strategic Earning Roadmap

Professor FinanceWise handed each friend a golden envelope. Inside: a Mini-CFO's Earning Strategy Map.

Your Map Includes:

- **Don't just find a job—seek opportunities** where you can learn, grow, and connect with people who help you reach your future goals in your dream industry or company.

Your first job might not be your dream role yet, but if it's in the right place, it's a smart place to start. You can prove yourself, build skills, and earn chances to move up by being creative and proactive about your growth.

- **Use today's work as a ladder**
  Each step (or gig) should get you higher—closer to what you want to learn or become.

- **Explore the future of work**
  Think beyond lemonade stands. Try:
  - Selling digital art
  - Starting a podcast
  - Freelancing online
  - Helping a small business with marketing

- **Always ask:**
  "Where could this lead me?"

Draw This!

Bella held up her drawing pad:
"Draw a Gig That Grows You."

First, sketch a job or hustle you can start today.
Then, sketch where it might lead you in 1 year… 3 years… 10 years!
Don't forget to add the *sparkly* things you'll learn or the people you'll meet along the way—those special moments that make your journey exciting!

Reflection Time — What We Learned

As the lesson ends, Professor FinanceWise shares one timeless truth about earning:

"Money is helpful, but strategy is powerful."

Key Takeaway for Kids

Earning with purpose builds confidence, develops skills, and opens doors to new opportunities.

Final Inspiration

"Even the smallest job can open the path to your biggest dreams."

Education Skills Savings

Doctor Dreams

Chapter 4

Two Roads to Wealth: Lessons in Education and Financial Intelligence

After hearing about the two different paths to wealth, Timmy the Tortoise and his friends began asking deeper questions. What role do education, skills, and money play in building a secure future? Professor Timeless Wisdom helps them explore answers that schools often skip.

Timmy the Tortoise, Bella the Bunny, Max the Monkey, and Lily the Ladybug were sitting near the Great Oak Tree on the edge of Prosperity Hollow, discussing what they wanted to be when they grew up.

"I want to be a doctor!" said Bella excitedly.

"I think I'd make a great inventor!" Max declared while balancing an hourglass on his tail.

"I want to be a teacher," Lily said, adjusting her tiny checklist.

Timmy, the wisest of the group, took a deep breath. "I'm not sure yet," he admitted. "But I want to learn how money works."

Just then, **Professor Timeless Wisdom**, the wise old owl, flew down and landed on his wooden stand.

"Ah, my young friends, that is a very important question. Would you like to hear a story about two very different people who learned about money in different ways?"

The four friends nodded eagerly.

Professor Timeless Wisdom looked at the four friends. "So, what do you think the lesson is?"

Bella raised her paw. "Education is important!"

"Absolutely," said the Professor. "Many studies show that **higher education leads to lower poverty and higher income for countries**. But what else?"

Max scratched his head. "The MBA was really smart, but he didn't take action."

"Exactly!" said the Professor. "He **waited too long**. The Dropout didn't have a degree, but he **used his skills and took action**."

Timmy adjusted his glasses. "So, the best thing to do is **get an education, learn skills, and save money early**?"

The Professor nodded. "That's right! If the MBA had saved money when he had a job, he wouldn't have been in financial trouble. And if he had learned how to start a business—and built a few practical skills to support it—he wouldn't have needed to depend only on jobs."

Lily smiled. "So, education is good, but we also need to learn about money, business, and saving."

"Indeed," said the Professor. "And that's exactly what we're going to learn together."

Reflection Time — What We Learned

As the friends reflected beneath the Great Oak Tree, Professor Timeless Wisdom shared one powerful truth:
"Education builds understanding, but financial intelligence and action build your future."

Key Takeaway for Kids

A strong foundation comes from learning, building practical skills, saving early, and taking action when opportunities appear.

Final Inspiration

"Knowledge opens doors — but action turns those doors into pathways."

Section 2:

The Pillars of Personal Finance

Theme: *Earning is only the beginning—this section explores the core money habits and decision-making psychology that shape a Mini-CFO's destiny. Children learn the pillars of smart saving, thoughtful spending, disciplined habits, and taking risks intelligently.*

Chapter 5

The Safety Net Saving Secret: How Smart Savers Stay Ready for Life's Surprises

Under the shade of the Great Oak Tree, the sun shimmered softly through the leaves as the four friends gathered again. Today, Max the Monkey was unusually quiet.

"What's wrong, Max?" asked Lily the Ladybug.

Max looked down at his empty pouch. "I spent all my lemonade stand money on the latest flying gadget. Now I don't have anything left to buy more lemons or cups!"

Professor Timeless Wisdom swooped down and perched on his wooden stand, just in time.

"Ah, a lesson in saving, I see," he said with a wise smile. "Let me tell you a story—not just about people, but about how even businesses must learn to **save** wisely."

The Story of Sara and the Smoothie Stand

Once upon a time, there was a clever young squirrel named Sara who ran a smoothie stand in Acorn Valley.

Business was booming. Every chipmunk and bunny came to her for fresh fruit smoothies after school. Sara made good profits and used them to decorate her stand with shiny signs, colorful umbrellas, and a nut-powered blender.

But Sara also did something smart — each week, she put 20% of her profits into a special jar labeled: **"Emergency & Growth Fund."**

Her friends teased her.
"Why not buy new gadgets instead?" they asked.

Sara shrugged. "What if something unexpected happens?"

Then one rainy week, a giant storm hit Acorn Valley. Her smoothie stand blew over, and all the cups and fruit supplies were gone.

"Oh no!" cried the customers. "No smoothies?"

But Sara smiled. "Give me one day!"

Thanks to her savings jar, she quickly rebuilt her stand, bought fresh fruit, and was back in business—faster than anyone else.

Professor Timeless Wisdom leaned forward and said, "Now let's look at how saving works in the real world — for families, workers, and even big businesses."

Real Life Can Be a Roller Coaster — Why Saving Matters More Than Ever

Just like Sara the Squirrel had a storm roll in out of nowhere, real life is full of unexpected twists and turns — even for grown-ups and big businesses.

Sometimes, people lose their jobs because their company has to shut down or the economy slows down. Sometimes, a big surprise—like a worldwide illness or a natural disaster—can make it hard for businesses to stay open or families to pay their bills.

In one town, there was a famous news company that was doing really well. Its founder had big dreams and kept reinvesting all the money into new ideas. But then, the economy changed. He didn't have enough savings to handle the tough times. Eventually, he had to give up the company he started.

In another city, when a sickness spread across the world, many people couldn't work for months. The ones who had savings made it through. The ones who didn't… really struggled. Some lost their homes, their shops, or had to borrow money just to eat.

That's why saving money is like **building an umbrella for rainy days** — you hope you don't need it, but when the storm comes, you'll be so glad it's there.

The truth is: **No one knows the future**. But with savings, you don't have to be afraid of it.

Now that the four friends understood how powerful saving could be in the real world, they were ready to hear more from Professor Timeless Wisdom.

Back at the Great Oak Tree

Professor Timeless Wisdom looked at Max.

"Now, Max, what do you think would've happened if Sara didn't save anything?"

Max scratched his head. "She would've been out of business for a long time."

"Exactly," said the Professor. "That's true for people and businesses. When you save, you protect your future."

Timmy nodded thoughtfully. "So saving isn't just about money—it's about being ready."

Bella raised her paw. "Can a business have a savings account like people do?"

"Absolutely!" said the Professor. "In business, we call it **'working capital'** or **'reserves.'** It helps pay for unexpected expenses or lets a business grow when the time is right."

"Some people borrow money from a bank instead of saving, but that can be risky. Loans always come with a cost—like interest—and if the business isn't doing well, the bank might not lend at all," said the Professor.

"In some cases, if the business can't pay back the loan, it may even lose part—or all—of its ownership. That's why saving is such a smart way to stay strong and independent," said the Professor.

Lily added, "So if we save a little now, we can do a lot more later!"

Reflection Time — What We Learned

As the friends listened, Professor Timeless Wisdom reminded them that saving isn't about having less today—it's about being ready for tomorrow. Just like Sara the Squirrel rebuilt her stand after the storm, savings give everyone the strength to rise again when life surprises them.

Key Takeaway for Kids

Saving—no matter how small—builds safety, confidence, and future opportunities. People save. Businesses save. And every little bit helps.

Final Inspiration

"Save a little. Stay ready. Shine bright."

Spending Leaks   Budget Fix   Savings Growth

Find Leaks
Fix Habits
Grow Wealth

Monthly
Expenses

Leak
List

Chapter 6

The Secret Superpower of Saving: Fix Leaks, Build Habits, Grow Wealth

A Story of Leaks and Lightbulbs

B ella was surprised when her Uncle Felix the Fox, a retired financial consultant, visited one evening. Sharp as ever, he had a reputation for helping families "find their leaks" — money they didn't even realize was being wasted.

He just said, **"Bring your bank and credit card statements. We're going leak-hunting."**

The family sat around the dining table. One by one, he pointed things out:

- A magazine subscription nobody read.

- A gym membership no one used.

- A $15 monthly donation to a church they hadn't visited in years.

- Three different video streaming services — all charging monthly fees.

"You'd be surprised," Uncle Felix the Fox smiled. **"Many people don't have a money problem. They have a leak problem**."

By the end of the evening, the family had found over **$240 in monthly money leaks**.

That's more than **$2,800 a year**, just draining away.

Bella whispered,
"That's a vacation. That's a college course. That's... a future."

And as the family looked at the total savings, something changed. They felt lighter. Less worried.

Bella smiled, "It feels good knowing we're in control."

Uncle Felix the Fox nodded:
"Exactly. Saving isn't about sacrifice. It's about freedom. It's about peace of mind."

Why Saving Is Harder Than It Looks

Saving isn't flashy. It's not exciting like shopping or investing in the next big stock. In fact, for many people, saving money is harder than climbing a mountain.

A recent report showed that:

- Over **60% of Americans** couldn't cover a **$1,000 emergency** without borrowing.

- Nearly **40% have less than $400** in their savings account.

Even many adults — with decent jobs — live paycheck to paycheck. Why?

Because **saving isn't just about money**. It's about **behavior, culture, and habit**.

Money Wisdom from Professor FinanceWise

"Saving is harder than a camel passing through the eye of a needle," said the Professor.
"But those who master it build bridges across deserts. They don't just survive — they thrive."

What Makes Saving So Powerful?

Saving does incredible things:

1. It Gives You Control

When you have savings:

- A broken laptop isn't a disaster.

- A job loss isn't a crisis.

- An opportunity isn't missed due to lack of cash.

"Money saved is peace earned." – The Professor

2. It Builds Your Future

Every dollar saved is a **seed**. And guess what happens when seeds grow?

The Hidden Magic of Compound Interest

Most people underestimate what a small habit can do over time. That's where **compound interest** comes in — the world's quiet superpower.

Let's break it down:

- **Simple interest**: You earn money on your savings.

- **Compound interest**: You earn money on your savings **and** the interest it earned earlier.

It's interest on interest. Like a snowball rolling down a hill, it grows faster and faster.

Story of Two Savers

Lily the Ladybug starts saving $10 a month at age 15.
Max the Monkey waits until he's 25, saving $25 a month.
They both stop saving at 40.

By retirement, Lily has more money — even though she saved less.

"Because Lily started earlier, her money had more time to grow and earn interest on interest — that's the magic of compounding!"

That's the power of time and compounding.

Compounding means your money earns interest… and then that interest also earns interest.

Want to see the magic of compounding in action?

Imagine this: You save **$1**, and it **doubles every 7 years**.

- After 7 years → $2
- After 14 years → $4
- After 21 years → $8
- After 28 years → **$16**

That's just one dollar!

Now imagine doing that with a few dollars every month, and for even longer. That's the power of *starting early*.

"You didn't do anything extra except wait and let your money grow!"

It's like planting a small tree early. With enough time, it grows big — giving shade, fruit, and freedom.

Even small savings, if started early, can grow into something amazing.

"Now imagine doing that with your birthday money, or the allowance you save up every month. Your small start could turn into something big—just by letting time help you!"

The Dark Side of the Same Power

Here's the twist: **Debt compounds too.** Just like your savings can grow... so can your debt.

- If you borrow $1,000 on a credit card at 20% interest and don't pay it back? It can **double in less than 4 years**.

"Compound interest is a double-edged sword. Wield it wisely — or it will cut you deeply."

What to Do With Your Savings?

Once you build the habit, your savings can:

- **Start a business**
- **Take you through a crisis** without panic
- **Pay for education** without loans
- **Help a loved one** when they need it
- Or simply let you **sleep better at night**
- Many other things that help you live with peace, purpose, and possibility.

And that's just the beginning. With savings, you gain choices — and with choices, you shape your future.

Professor's Challenge

Professor Timeless Wisdom smiled at the friends.
"Imagine your savings as a tiny tree," he said. "Every coin you save helps it grow."

Try This:

- 🌱 **After a week:** What does your little money-tree look like?

- 🌿 **After a month:** How much has it grown?

- 🌳 **After a year:** How tall and strong is it now?

"Draw it, imagine it, or just picture it in your mind," said the Professor.
"Your savings grow just like a living tree — little by little."

Professor's Exercise

Professor Timeless Wisdom gave the friends a simple challenge:

"Find the leaks. Fix the pipe."

This week, look through your (or your family's) bank or card statements:

- Are there subscriptions you don't use?

- Can you switch to a cheaper option?

- Are there small expenses you can pause?

Every dollar you save is a dollar you control.

Reflection Time — What We Learned

Professor Timeless Wisdom reminded the friends that saving isn't just about keeping money—it's about choosing a future with strength, freedom, and possibility. When we protect our money from leaks and grow it wisely, even small habits turn into something powerful.

Key Takeaway for Kids

Saving smart means more than earning—it means keeping, protecting, and growing what you already have.

Final Inspiration

"Fix the leaks. Build the habit. Grow your future."

Chapter 7

The Smart Spender's Secret: How to Get the Most From Your Money

The Store Temptation

The friends stood in front of a giant, glittering store window. Max the Monkey was glued to the glass.

"Look at that SUPER LAUNCHER LASER BLASTER!" Max said, his eyes wide. "I *need* it!"

"Max," Bella said gently, "didn't you say the same thing about the glitter-goggles last week?"

"That was different," Max muttered. "These have sound effects."

Just then, Professor FinanceWise stepped in, smiling.

"Ah, the **power of spending**. Shall we learn how to use it wisely?"

What Is Smart Spending?

Professor gathered the friends around.

"Saving is important," he said, "but how you *spend* is just as powerful."

"Every coin is like a vote," said Timmy. "You're telling the world what matters to you."

Smart spending isn't about **never buying anything fun**.
It's about **making your money count** — for the things that **truly matter to you**.

The 3 Golden Rules of Smart Spending

1. Think Before You Buy

Ask: Do I *really* need this? Will I still love it next week?

2. Spend on Purpose, Not Pressure

Don't let ads, peer pressure, or FOMO make the decision for you.

3. Every Coin Has a Job

Assign your money to your goals — fun today, freedom tomorrow.

A True Story: The Clerk and the Manager

Bella raised her paw.

"Professor, my cousin told me a story about her old office. There was a kind clerk named Anita. She didn't earn a lot, but she was careful. She avoided buying things just because they were trendy. Instead, she saved for what really mattered."

"And then there was her manager," Bella continued. "He had a big salary and bought the newest of *everything*. He called it 'living large.'"

Years passed. Both retired.

Anita, the clerk, had **more savings, more peace, and more choices.**
The manager? He had stories, but not much money left.

"It's not about how much you earn," said Professor Timeless, nodding. "It's about *how* you spend."

Ready to decide if that next buy is really worth it?

Try This: The "Joy-per-Dollar" Test

Before buying something, ask:

- Will this bring me joy that lasts?

- Is it worth the time it took me to earn this?

Max figured out his toy would cost 4 hours of banana-delivery work.

(That's how Max imagines his chores paying for his toys — banana delivery!)

"Oof," he said. "Maybe not."

Avoid the Spending Traps

Watch out for:

- **Impulse Buying**: "It's on sale!" (But do you need it?) Example: If you buy a toy on sale for $10, but never play with it, that's $10 wasted!

- **Emotional Shopping**: Feeling bored or sad? Don't let your money handle your emotions.

- **Comparison Game**: Just because someone else bought it doesn't mean you should too.

Professor's Exercise: Draw This!

Imagine your wallet is a backpack.
You can only carry the things that truly matter.

Let's find out what's worth keeping!

1. **Draw 5 things** you bought or want — that you *truly love and use often*.

2. **Now draw 5 things** you bought but *barely ever used*.

3. **Look at both pictures.**
   Ask yourself:
   "What would Smart Me choose next time?"

The Smart Spender always thinks before they pack their money-backpack.

Did You Know?

The rules of smart spending don't just apply to people.
Businesses, **cities**, and even **whole countries** can get into serious trouble when they spend more than they have.

Some fall into deep debt. Some go bankrupt.
Others lose the freedom to make their own decisions — because they owe too much to others.

That's why smart spending isn't just smart — it's **powerful**.

When you learn to spend wisely, you're practicing a skill that even the biggest organizations *need but sometimes forget*.

And you're giving yourself something money can't buy: **peace of mind**.

Level Up: Big Picture Thinking

Smart spending means:

- You still have fun.

- But you skip the clutter.

- And your money *builds* your dreams.

Every smart spender is a **mini-CEO of their money.**
You're the boss. Make it work *for you*.

Wise Words from Professor Timeless Wisdom

"When you spend with your *head* and your *heart*, your money becomes your sidekick — not your boss."

Reflection Time — What We Learned

Professor Timeless Wisdom reminded the friends that smart spending isn't about saying "no" to fun—it's about saying "yes" to the things that truly matter. Every choice we make with our money shapes our habits, our confidence, and our future freedom.

Key Takeaway for Kids

Smart spending means thinking before buying, avoiding pressure, and choosing what brings real value. When you give every coin a purpose, your money starts working for *you*.

Final Inspiration

"Spend with intention. Choose with clarity. Build the future you imagine."

GOOD DECISIONS =
INFORMATION + STRATEGY

Wisdom Hill
1 DEFINE
2 GATHER
3 COMPAR
4 DECIDE
5 REVIE

Chapter 8

The Thinking Tree: A Lesson in Wise Decisions

The four friends gathered beneath a large, shady tree on the edge of Prosperity Hollow. Its wide branches, twisting roots, and whispering leaves made it their favorite meeting spot.

Professor Timeless Wisdom adjusted his hat and said,
"Welcome to the Thinking Tree — the perfect place to talk about one of the most powerful tools in life and business: **decision-making**."

What Is Decision-Making, Really?

Max wiggled his tail. "You mean like choosing which ice cream to get?"

The Professor chuckled. "That's right, Max! Every time you choose between two or more options — you're making a decision. But in business, decisions often involve bigger questions — like how to spend money, what product to launch, or who to hire. That's why we need more than just guesses."

Lily nodded. "So… no eeny-meeny-miny-mo?"

"Not if you want your business to survive," said the Professor. "We aim for *informed* decisions — choices backed by facts, not just feelings."

The Magic Formula: Good Decisions = Information + Strategy

Bella raised a paw. "What do you mean by '**informed**'?"

"Well," said the Professor, "imagine you want to open a lemonade stand. Would you just guess where to set it up, or would you check which corner gets more foot traffic?"

"I'd check!" said Timmy.
"Exactly," replied the Professor. "That's informed decision-making — using real information to choose the best option."

Lily tapped her notepad. "And you said something about **strategy**?"

"Yes! Strategy means seeing the *big picture*. It's like using a map instead of wandering. Strategic thinking asks:

- Where are we going?

- What resources do we have?
- What might go wrong?
- What's the best path forward?"

"You want to make decisions based on information and clarity — not confusion or pressure. Good decisions come from good thinking — not guessing or rushing," said the Professor.

Feelings ≠ Facts

"Sometimes," said the Professor, "people make decisions based on emotions — fear, excitement, pride. But in business, that's dangerous."

"Why?" asked Max.

"Because feelings change. But facts are steady. Let's say a company buys a new building just because the CEO *loves* how it looks — but didn't check the price or location. That's not smart. It could hurt the company."

Bella frowned. "So feelings don't matter at all?"

"Oh, they matter," the Professor smiled. "But they should never **control** your decisions. Feelings can guide you to ask better questions — but let logic lead the way."

Think Deeply — Then Act Boldly

Professor Timeless Wisdom paused under the tree and said,
"There's a saying — smart decision-makers spend *90% of their time understanding the problem,* and only *10% finding the solution.* The deeper you understand what's really going on, the better your decisions will be."

Timmy's eyes lit up. "So it's like solving a puzzle! If I rush, I might miss the corner pieces."

"Exactly," said the Professor. "Wise leaders slow down just enough to think clearly — then they act with purpose."

Bella's Story: The Backpack Decision

Bella looked thoughtful. "I remember when I had two backpacks to choose from — one was flashy and fun, the other strong and waterproof. I wanted the flashy one *so badly*! But I thought about our hikes and how often it rains. So I chose the sturdy one."

"Excellent decision-making," said the Professor. "You thought about **function**, not just **feelings**. That's wisdom in action."

What Good Decision-Making Looks Like

Lily summarized it beautifully on the board:

1. **Define the problem.**
   What are you trying to solve?

2. **Gather information.**
   What do you know — and what do you *need* to know?

3. **List your options.**
   What paths can you take?

4. **Weigh the pros and cons.**
   What are the possible outcomes of each?

5. **Make the best decision you can — with the information you have.**

6. **Review and learn.**
   Even if things don't go perfectly, ask: What did I learn?

Professor's Final Words

"In business, every decision is critical because it involves scarce resources — like money, time, and energy. That's why smart decision-making is at the heart of being a Mini CFO."

"Management," said the Professor, "is really decision-making in action. The word *manage* comes from handling situations *tactfully*. Great managers — and great business leaders — don't just work hard. They think hard."

"They *see the big picture*, look at the facts, and choose wisely. Then they act. And if they learn something new, they adapt. That's how smart decisions shape strong futures."

Reflection Time — What We Learned

Under the Thinking Tree, Professor Timeless Wisdom reminded the friends that great decisions aren't accidents—they're built through clarity, information, and calm thinking. When we pause, gather facts, and see the bigger picture, we give ourselves the power to choose our future instead of being pushed by pressure or emotion.

Key Takeaway for Kids

Wise decision-making begins with understanding the problem, asking smart questions, and letting facts lead the way. Good choices today become strong opportunities tomorrow.

Final Inspiration

"Think deeply. Choose wisely. Lead boldly."

SMART RISK FORMULA

TRUTH + THOUGHTFULNESS
+ TIMING + TINY TEST
= SMART RISK

Go Smart, Not Fast!

Study ☐
Save ☐
Safety ☐

PLAN A

Courage is good — but only with prepara
wisdom, and a plan.

Chapter 9

Jump... But With a Parachute! — The Art of Taking Smart Risks

The Leap at Parachute Cliff

The four friends were back in the Learning Grove with Professor Timeless Wisdom, who stood today in front of a large picture titled: **"Parachute Cliff — Take the Leap, But Land Smart!"**

"Woah," said Max, eyes wide. "Is that for skydiving?"

"Not quite," the Professor chuckled. "But it's a perfect picture of what we're learning today — *smart risks*!"

What Is a Risk?

Lily raised a wing. "Professor, what *is* a risk?"

"Great question," he said. "A risk is when you **do something uncertain**, and it might go really well… or not. Like trying a new recipe, entering a race, or starting a business. Risks are part of life — and part of finance too."

Calculated Risk vs. Careless Risk

"Let me show you two friends," said the Professor, pulling down a new chart.

1. Meet Sam: The Risk Calculator

Sam had saved up **$2,500** from helping at the community garden and doing graphic design on weekends. He loved futuristic tech and had a curiosity about robots — even though he wasn't a programmer yet.

One day, he studied a robotics company called **NovaChips**. Most people ignored it — the stock price was low, and the news wasn't exciting. But Sam noticed something others didn't. The company had **brilliant engineers**, **smart patents**, and was quietly building tools that powered innovation across industries.

Sam invested **$500** — just 20% of his savings. It was an amount he could afford to lose.

"That's a *calculated and affordable risk*," said Professor Timeless Wisdom. "He didn't gamble. He studied. He stayed calm. And he only risked what he could afford to lose."

Over the next 10 years, **NovaChips** soared. Stock splits, product launches, and global adoption helped Sam's $500 investment grow into **over $1 million**.

2. Meet Ray: The Risk Taker

Ray sold his entire lemonade stand and used the entire money to invest in a shiny new internet company called **"FastLine"**.

"He didn't really study the company," said the Professor. "He just heard it was going to be 'huge.' He hoped to triple his money fast."

"But FastLine failed. Ray lost it all. And he had no parachute — no savings left."

That's Why We Say: Jump... But With a Parachute!

"Taking risks is not bad," said the Professor. "In fact, it's **part of being a smart Mini CFO**. But the key is..."

"Take affordable risks — the kind that won't break you if they don't go well."

The CFO Way: Risk is Part of the Job!

"Did you know **CFOs — Chief Financial Officers** — take risks every day?" asked the Professor. "They make decisions about:

- Where to invest,
- Which projects to fund,
- How to manage cash, and
- How to plan for the future.

"But they don't flip coins. They study the numbers. They look at different paths. They calculate. That's called..."

"informed risk-taking."

One More Inspiring Story...

Bella's ears perked up.

"There was once someone who saved **a little bit every year**, studied great companies, and invested through something called a **Roth IRA**," said the Professor.

"What's that?" asked Timmy.

"A special account where your money grows, and later you **don't pay taxes when you withdraw it at retirement** — if you follow the rules."

"This person didn't rush. Didn't guess. Just saved and invested wisely. By retirement, they had **millions — and no tax bill!**"

That's the magic of a Roth IRA," said the Professor. "Even ordinary people who invest consistently can grow tax-free wealth over time — some have even turned small investments into millions."

"There are even rare cases where early investments in high-growth private companies grew into billions — all tax-free inside a Roth IRA. While that's extremely uncommon, it shows what's possible when long-term vision meets smart choices. Who knows? One of you might someday write your own remarkable story. Your saving habits, decision-making, financial intelligence, calculated risks, and timely actions could make all the difference."

"Stock investing is just one way to grow wealth over time," said the Professor. "That was just one example.

People also build wealth in many other ways — like starting small businesses, saving regularly in bank accounts, investing in fixed deposits, or even buying gold. Of course, each of these comes with its own risks — theft, inflation, or even business failure.

But the key isn't what you choose. It's how you think. Learn the rules, take calculated risks, and stay calm. That's how real builders grow wealth."

The Magic Formula of Smart Risk

The Professor wrote this on the board:

Truth + Thoughtfulness + Timing + Tiny Test = Smart Risk

"Let's break that down," he said:

- **Truth** → Find facts. Study before you jump.

- **Thoughtfulness** → Don't rush. Think it through.

- **Timing** → Jump at the right moment.

- **Tiny Test** → Try small first. Can you afford to lose that part?

And Remember...

"Jumping is part of growing," said the Professor. "But always pack your parachute — a plan, a backup, and wisdom."

Professor's Final Words

"Don't be afraid to dream big — just be smart about how you leap.
Not every big win comes from a big risk.
But every smart win comes from a smart plan."

Reflection Time — What We Learned

Under the Learning Grove, Professor Timeless Wisdom reminded the friends that risk isn't something to fear — it's something to understand. Smart risks are built on facts, planning, and calm thinking. When you prepare your parachute before you leap, even uncertain paths become opportunities.

Key Takeaway for Kids

Smart risk-taking means studying the facts, starting small, and only risking what you can afford to lose. With patience, learning, and strategy, even tiny steps can grow into something remarkable.

Final Inspiration

"Think smart. Start small. Leap wisely."

Disclaimer

This book is for educational purposes only. Investing, business, and financial decisions involve risk. Always speak with a trusted adult or qualified financial advisor before making real-life financial choices.

Section 3:

The Business Brain of a Mini-CFO

Theme: *From money manager to value creator — this section helps children understand how real businesses work. Through simple models and engaging stories, young readers learn core business operations, the accounting equation, budgeting, profit analysis, ratios, and how internal auditing protects a company's financial health.*

EVERY BUSINESS HAS AN EQUATION!
ASSETS = LIABILITIES + CAPITAL
+ REVENUE - EXPENSES - WITHDRAWALS

ASSETS
LIABILITIES
CAPITAL
REVENUE
EXPENSES
WITHDRAWALS

Sell
Lemonade

Buy Lemons
(Expenses)

(Reven

Capital

Profit

Assets

Our
Business Assets
= $80
LEMONADE

Chapter 10

The Equation That Runs Every Business

A Mini-CFO Adventure into Income,
Expenses, Capital & More

A Walk, a Question, and a Challenge

One sunny morning, Bella the Bunny, Max the Monkey, Lily the Ladybug, and Timmy the Tortoise met Professor FinanceWise for another exciting mission.

"I'm ready to run the best lemonade stand ever — *using fresh, organic, forest-grown lemons*!" Max exclaimed.

"Let's track everything!" Lily said, holding up her notepad.

"Let's make it official. We're a business now," Timmy added.

Professor FinanceWise smiled.
"Then you must think like a **Mini-CFO**—someone who understands how a business truly works, not just what it sells."

The Shopkeeper's Secret

At the market, near Prosperity Hollow, two shopkeepers were arguing.

"You forgot the accounting equation!" one said.
"You're not tracking your business right!" said the other.

The friends looked puzzled.

"What's the **accounting equation**?" Bella whispered.

Professor FinanceWise adjusted his spectacles.
"Ah, that's your challenge today. It's time to uncover how the **money side** of business works!"

Step One: A Quick Reminder from Last Time

The Professor drew the **basic formula** in the air:

Assets = Liabilities + Equity

"This shows what a business owns, what it owes, and what belongs to the owner," he said. "You've seen this before—it's the **core structure** of business."

"But businesses do more than just exist," Lily said. "They sell stuff, buy things, and pay for lemons!"

"Exactly," the Professor nodded. "So now it's time to see the **whole picture**."

Seeing the Flow — Not Just the Formula

The Professor paused and said:

"This equation doesn't show how to squeeze lemons or hand out cups — it shows how **money moves** in and out of a business. It tells you:

- what you **own**

- what you **owe**

- how much you've **earned**

- what you've **spent**

- and whether you made **profit or loss**.

Like a map, it shows where your money is and how your business is doing."

Lily's eyes widened. "It's like the business's brain!"

"Or backbone," Timmy added.

"Or a treasure map!" Max laughed.

Thinking Like a Mini-CFO

The Professor wrote each term clearly on the board:

- **Assets** – What your business owns (like cash, ingredients, tables).

- **Liabilities** – What your business owes (loans, unpaid bills).

- **Owner's Capital** – What you invest or contribute to start or grow the business.

- **Revenue** – Money the business earns by selling products or services.

- **Expenses** – Costs of running the business (like lemons, signs, rent).

- **Withdrawals** – Money taken out by the owner for personal use.
- **Net Income (or Net Loss)** – The result after subtracting all expenses from revenue.

If revenue is more than expenses, it's a **profit**.
If expenses are more than revenue, it's a **loss**.

The Big Picture — The Extended Equation

Professor FinanceWise grinned and revealed:

Assets = Liabilities + Capital + Revenue – Expenses – Withdrawals

"This is how the money flows," he said. "This is how a CFO sees the business."

"It's like a dashboard for the whole company!" Lily said.

"Exactly," the Professor nodded.

"It's not just what you have—it's how you got it, and what's **changing**. This equation shows whether your business is **growing or shrinking**."

Mini-CFO Insight: Accrual vs. Cash Accounting

Most big companies (and many small ones) use the **accrual basis of accounting**, which means they record income **when it is earned** and expenses **when they are incurred**, even if no money has changed hands yet. That's how we get accurate profit numbers using the accounting equation. The **cash basis**, on the other hand, records money only when it comes in or goes out. While cash basis is simple and sometimes used for very small businesses or tax reporting, **the accrual method is considered more accurate** for understanding how a business is really performing.

The Lemonade Stand Example

The Professor handed out a **business summary sheet** of their lemonade stand transactions — a simple list of what they earned, spent, and invested — so they could **tally the accounting equation** like real Mini-CFOs.

- Each friend invests $10 = **Capital = $40**

- They earn $60 from lemonade sales = **Revenue = $60**

- They spend $20 on ingredients = **Expenses = $20**

- No money borrowed = **Liabilities = $0**

- No money taken out = **Withdrawals = $0**

Equation:

Assets = 0 (Liabilities) + 40 (Capital) + 60 (Revenue) – 20 (Expenses) – 0 (Withdrawals)
Assets = **$80**

"And notice— the $80 in assets equals the other side of the equation. Both sides always balance, because every business transaction affects two places. That's the magic of double-entry — the system all real businesses follow," said the Professor.

"We'll explore how that works in just a moment," he added with a wink.

"Boom! You now have $80 in business assets."

"We're rich!" Max jumped.

"No," Bella laughed, "We're **smart!**"

"And smarter still," Professor FinanceWise added,
"because now you know the same secret **every big company** uses: the **accounting equation!**
It **tracks money** — where it comes from, where it goes, and what's left. That's how business success is measured."

A Hidden Secret: Why the Equation Works

"But wait," Lily asked, "how does it always stay balanced?"

"Great question!" said the Professor. "It works because of something called the **double-entry system.**"

"Double-entry?" Timmy tilted his head.

Professor FinanceWise smiled and drew a tiny see-saw in the air.
"Every time money moves in a business; it touches **two places**—that's the secret."

Then he gave an example:

"Let's say you buy lemons for $5:
- You lose $5 in **cash** (an asset goes down),
- At the same time, your **expenses** go up by $5 (which reduces net income)."

"That's two places!" said Bella.

"Exactly," the Professor nodded. "Every entry has a **partner entry**. That's why it's called double-entry. It ensures that the accounting equation always stays balanced — just like a perfectly level see-saw."

"Can you give us another one?" Max asked, scratching his head.

"Of course!" said the Professor.

"Let's say you sell lemonade and earn $10:
- Your **cash** (an asset) goes up by $10,
- And your **revenue** increases by $10 (which boosts net income, and grows your equity)."

"So… selling or spending always changes two things?" Max asked.

"Exactly," said the Professor. "That's how every business — big or small — keeps track of money. It's not just numbers; it's a **smart system** that's been working for **hundreds of years all around the world**."

"So it's like a magic rule for tracking everything," Max grinned.

"Not magic," the Professor winked, "just **smart accounting!**"

Why Mini-CFOs Need This

The Professor gathered the friends for one last thought.

"Understanding this equation is like seeing the **skeleton of the business** — the inner structure that holds everything together. It's not about selling lemonade or counting lemons. It's about knowing where the money **comes from**, where it **goes**, and where it **is now**."

"It shows whether your business is **growing or shrinking**, whether you're **earning or losing**, and whether you're **spending wisely** or wasting resources. Every number tells part of the story — and when you understand how they all connect, you see the **big picture**."

Bella nodded. "So, it's like having X-ray vision for a business."

"Exactly," the Professor smiled.
"It helps you **think like a CFO** — or maybe even a future CEO."

Max stood taller. "Or both!"

Professor's Final Words

The Professor looked at the four friends, proud.

"Are you ready to take on your own business challenge?"

Timmy, Bella, Max, and Lily all raised their hands.

"Then let's go build something amazing — with numbers that speak louder than words."

And just like that, their Mini-CFO journey had only just begun.

The Ultimate Accounting Equation

Basic Accounting Equation

Assets = Liabilities + Equity

Expanded Accounting Equation

Assets = Liabilities + Capital + Revenue – Expenses – Withdrawals

Where Retained Earnings = Revenue – Expenses – Dividends

And, Revenue – Expenses = Net Income (or Net Loss)

Term	Definition
Assets	Resources owned by the business (cash, inventory, equipment).
Liabilities	What the business owes (loans, accounts payable).
Equity	Owner's claim on the business after liabilities are paid.
Capital	Owner's investment into the business.
Revenue	Income earned from selling goods/services.
Expenses	Costs incurred to earn revenue.
Withdrawals	Money taken out by the owner for personal use.
Retained Earnings	Accumulated profits not distributed as dividends.
Dividends	Profits distributed to owners/shareholders.

Skillful Adventures™

Reflection Time — What We Learned

Professor FinanceWise reminded the friends that the accounting equation isn't just math — it's the framework that lets every business in the world tell its story. When you understand where money comes from, where it goes, and how it changes, you can see the true health of any business, big or small.

Key Takeaway for Kids

Every business decision leaves a trail in the equation. When you track assets, liabilities, capital, revenue, and expenses clearly, you gain "X-ray vision" into how a business grows — and you start thinking like a real Mini-CFO.

Final Inspiration

"See the numbers. Understand the story. Lead with clarity."

Chapter 11

Budget Like a Mini-CFO

Under the Great Mango Tree on the edge of Prosperity Hollow, Max sketched numbers in the dirt while Bella laid out maps. Lily arrived with berries, and Timmy snoozed nearby. Suddenly, Professor FinanceWise called, "Mini-CFOs, it's time to plan our forest business!"

"A Mini-CFO doesn't just count coins — they create plans, prepare for storms, and help the whole forest grow," he added.

What Is a Budget?

"**Budgeting**," said Professor FinanceWise, "isn't just about saying 'yes' or 'no' to spending. It's about **planning your journey**, making wise choices, and preparing for surprises. A good budget tells your money where to go—*before* it disappears!"

He drew a simple formula:

Earnings – Savings – Spending – Giving = What's Left to Grow!

"This helps you see where your money goes and how much is left to grow your future," said Professor.

"Remember, Mini-CFOs, setting your goals helps guide every coin you earn and spend!"

Woodland Business Budget Challenge

The team had just launched their new forest-side business:

🧻 *Timber & Treasures Cooperative* — selling:

- 🌳 Sustainable timber and furniture scraps
- 🍄 Gourmet mushrooms and healing herbs
- 🍓 Wild berries and natural resins
- 🐾 Nature walks and biodiversity credits

"Let's budget our month," said Bella, pulling out their Woodland Ledger.

Strategic Budgeting Scenarios

Scenario 1: The Big Mushroom Order

- **Offer:** A trader arrives and offers 100 forest coins for a shipment of rare mushrooms.

- **Choices**: Should everyone gather only mushrooms and risk having no berries or resins to sell, or split their efforts for steadier income?

- **Mini-CFO Solution:** Bella proposes splitting the harvest—60% mushrooms, 40% berries and resins—to balance high reward with safety. Max points out that rain is coming, and Lily reminds the team to have backup products.

- **Lesson:** Smart budgeting means planning for risk and considering what you might miss when you choose one thing over another (opportunity cost).

Encourage kids: 'Every coin is a decision—grow your forest and your future!'

Scenario 2: Rainy Season Incoming

- **Issue:** Dark clouds gather—storms approaching
  Mini-CFO Thinking: Mushrooms rot in rain; resins and furniture scraps don't
  Action: Shift goals to rain-resistant products

- **Lesson:** Adapt budgets using forecasting, making sure their business can thrive, rain or shine.

Team Budgeting & Negotiation

Let's set aside coins for replanting and emergencies," Bella suggests.

They vote and update their Monthly Forest Budget.

Mini-CFO Dashboard

Here's how our team tracks their progress every month to see how well they stick to their plan:

Goal	Target	Actual	Notes
Baskets Sold	20	18	Rain delayed two collections
Coins Saved	40	45	Saved more by cutting snacks
Replanting Fund	10% of income	Met	Ready for new saplings
Emergency Tools	5% of income	Not Met	Deferred to next month

"Dashboards show not just what you spent, but how well you stuck to your plan."
– Professor FinanceWise

Advanced Mini-CFO Lessons

Professor FinanceWise gathered the friends under the Great Mango Tree and said:

"Now that you understand how money moves through a business, it's time to learn how real CFOs think. These lessons will help you make wiser choices — whether you're running a lemonade stand or a forest business."

He wrote four ideas on a big wooden board:

1. Every choice costs something.
"Whenever you choose one thing, you give up another. That's called *opportunity cost.*
If you spend three coins on berries, that's three coins you can't save or invest."

2. Weather changes — plan for it.
"In business, storms can appear suddenly. That's why Mini-CFOs forecast — they think ahead and prepare."

3. Save today to grow tomorrow.
"Strong businesses reinvest. They save part of their earnings to buy better tools, more seeds, or bigger ideas."

4. Great decisions are made together.

"Teams talk. Teams plan. Teams negotiate. Listening to others helps you make smarter choices."

The friends nodded. Today, they weren't just learning numbers — they were learning how to *think like leaders.*

Professor's Big-Picture Inspiration Quote

Professor FinanceWise placed his hand on the mango tree and said:

"A Mini-CFO plans for today, invests for tomorrow, and grows with nature."

The friends smiled. The forest seemed to glow a little brighter.

Boardroom Pitch Challenge

Professor FinanceWise clapped his hands excitedly.

"Now it's your turn! Every great CFO knows how to explain their plan to others.
So here's your challenge…"

Pitch Your Budget!

"Present your monthly budget to your class or family.
Tell them:

- How many coins you earned

- How much you saved

- What you invested in

- And how you're planning for next month

If you can *explain* your money, you can *master* it."

Max puffed out his chest. "We're going to be the best forest CFOs ever!"

Mini-CFO Toolkit — Your Woodland Budget Sheet

Professor FinanceWise rolled out a parchment scroll.

"This," he said, "is your official Mini-CFO budget sheet.

Use it every month to track your coins and grow your forest business wisely."

Category	What goes here?	Amount (Coins)
⊚ Income	All coins you earn (sales, chores, jobs)	_____
🏛 Savings	Coins set aside for a goal or rainy day	_____
🌱 Reinvestment	Money used to buy better tools or more seeds	_____
🧺 Supplies	Money spent on baskets, tools, and business needs	_____
🌿 Giving	Coins shared to help others or support the forest	_____
🎉 Fun Fund	Money for treats, snacks, or celebration activities	_____
🚨 Emergency Reserve	Set aside just in case something unexpected happens	_____

How to Use:

1. **List your Income:** How many coins did you earn this month?

2. **Set Savings Goals:** How much do you want to save? (Aim for at least 20%!)

3. **Plan for Reinvestment:** What will help your business grow in the future — new tools, seeds, or training?

4. **Track Supplies:** What do you need to keep business running smoothly?

5. **Remember Giving:** Share some coins to help a friend, the forest, or a good cause.

6. **Add Fun Fund:** Plan for fun so you celebrate your hard work!

7. **Build Emergency Reserve:** Save a little for the "just in case" moments.

Fill out your Mini-CFO Toolkit every month. See which category is growing—and how your smart choices help your woodland business (and your future) thrive!

Bella's Question: Are We Becoming Real CFOs?

Bella:
"So… we're basically becoming real CFOs, right?"

Professor FinanceWise *(smiling)*:
"Almost! But remember — even grown-up CFOs learn every day. Business changes. Seasons shift. Smart minds adapt."

Max:
"Wait—there are different *kinds* of budgets too?"

Professor FinanceWise:
"Absolutely. Each one is like a different map for your money. Let me show you a few…"

Types of Budgets — Explained the Mini-CFO Way

- **Fixed Budget** – "Same amount every time."

- **Flexible Budget** – "Changes with the season."

- **Zero-Based Budget** – "Every coin gets a job."

- **Surplus Budget** – "Extra to save or invest."

- **Deficit Budget** – "Spent too much—how do we fix it?"

Professor FinanceWise:

"No matter which budget style you use, the parts of a budget usually stay the same — income, expenses, savings, and future plans. Let's break it down like a Mini-CFO!"

Budget Categories for Mini-CFOs

Budget Category	What It Means
Income	Money earned from business
Spending	Money for supplies and fun
Saving	Money set aside for goals
Investing	Money to make the business grow
Giving	Help the team or community
Reinvesting	Upgrade tools or expand sales

Max: "So, we track income, expenses, savings, and investing every time?"

Professor FinanceWise: "Yes! It's your dashboard to steer the business."

Reflection Time — What We Learned

The friends discovered that budgeting is more than tracking coins — it's a way of thinking. A budget gives you control, prepares you for surprises, and helps you choose wisely between today's wants and tomorrow's growth.
A Mini-CFO doesn't wait to see what happens—they plan the path, adjust for storms, and guide their business with clarity.

Key Takeaway for Kids

A strong budget tells your money where to go.
When you plan your income, savings, spending, and reinvestment, you're not just managing coins — you're building a future with confidence, teamwork, and smart decision-making.

Final Inspiration

"Plan with purpose. Save with vision. Grow with wisdom."

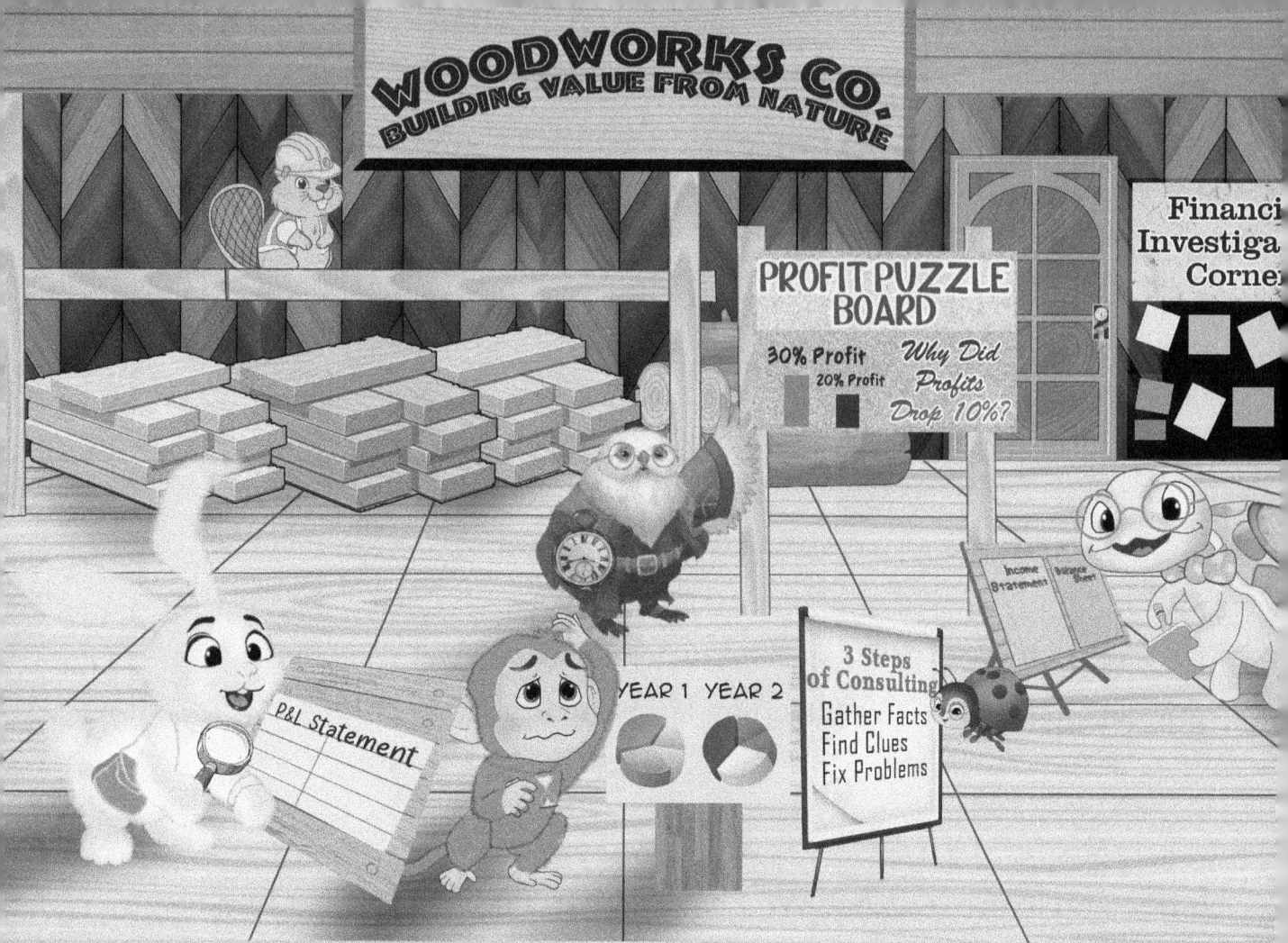

Chapter 12

❦

The Profit Puzzle at WoodWorks Co.

The forest was quiet — too quiet.

That's when Professor FinanceWise called an urgent meeting at his treehouse.

The Mysterious Drop in Profits

Professor FinanceWise: "Team, I just received a message from *WoodWorks Co.* They make wood panels, paper, and pulp — and they're struggling. The owner thinks everything's fine… but the profits have fallen 10% this year. He can't figure out why."

Max the Monkey: "Wait, the profits dropped, but he doesn't know what went wrong?"

Lily the Ladybug: "Sounds like a mystery for… the *Mini-CFO Consulting Team!*"

"Consulting means helping a business solve problems by asking questions, studying the numbers, and giving advice to make things better," said the Professor.

Bella the Bunny: "Let's go. We'll get our goggles, graphs, and gut instincts!"

Soon, the team hopped into the **Data Glider** and soared to the *WoodWorks* factory near the old riverbend.

Inside WoodWorks Co.

Logs rolled. Machines buzzed. But the mood felt heavy.

Owner (Mr. Elm): "Thank you for coming. I swear we worked hard this year. Costs seem okay. Sales look decent. But… profits are down 10%. I just don't get it."

Professor FinanceWise: "Let's find out together. Do you have the last two years of financials?"

Mr. Elm: "Yes, but… it's kind of messy."

Professor: "Perfect. Consultants love messy."

The 3-Step Consulting Process

Professor FinanceWise:
"Consultants usually follow three steps:

1. **Gather the facts**

2. **Find the hidden problems**

3. **Share advice to improve the business**

A consultant is like a detective for businesses — they look for clues in the numbers, figure out what's really happening, and then suggest smart fixes."

Mr. Elm handed over printed copies of the **Profit & Loss (P&L)**, **Balance Sheets**, and **Cash Flow Statements**.

Understanding Common-Size Math

Professor FinanceWise: "Let's begin with the P&L. We'll do something called a *Common-Size Income Statement*."

"Common-size means we show every line as a **% of revenue** — so we can compare across years, even if total dollars are different," explained Lily.

Bella ran her calculator while Max created the common-size chart using the numbers Mr. Elm provided from the past two years of financial statements.

WoodWorks Co. — Common-Size Income Statement (2-Year Snapshot)

Item	Amount (20XX)	% of Revenue (20XX)	Amount (20XY)	% of Revenue (20XY)
Revenue	$100,000	100%	$120,000	100%
Wood Raw Materials	$30,000	30%	$36,000	30%
Labor Costs	$25,000	25%	$30,000	25%
Energy & Utilities	$10,000	10%	$12,000	10%
Packaging	$5,000	5%	$6,000	5%
Net Profit	$30,000	**30%**	$24,000	**20%**

Mini-CFO Notes: What the Numbers Tell Us

- Percentages are calculated as a share of each year's total revenue to allow for year-over-year trend analysis.

- Costs remained **stable as a percentage of revenue**, but **net profit margin declined from 30% to 20%** — possibly due to **lower pricing** or changes in **sales mix or volume**.

- This format helps consultants visually compare business performance over time and spot trends in efficiency or margin improvement.

Professor FinanceWise smiled. "Excellent work, Mini-CFOs — you prepared the common-size statements yourself. That's exactly how real consultants and CFOs analyze financial performance."

Professor FinanceWise's Tip: Why Use Common-Size Columns?

"Common-size columns are always built using **your own math** — they don't appear in company reports. This is how consultants and CFOs make smart comparisons over time."

Lily the Ladybug:
"Professor, do we also do common-size for balance sheets?"

Professor:
"Absolutely! But instead of dividing by revenue, we divide every line by **total assets**. That shows how much cash, equipment, or debt a business has *compared to its full size!*"

What Is a Common-Size Balance Sheet?

A Common-Size Balance Sheet shows each item as a percentage of the company's total assets. This helps us understand how the business's money is spread out — what's tied up in cash, equipment, or owed to others. It also reveals the mix of debt and owner's equity used to fund the company.

By turning numbers into percentages, we can compare companies of different sizes or track changes over time — just like a Mini-CFO consultant!

The friends prepared a Common-Size Balance Sheet from the statements provided by Mr. Elm.

WoodWorks Co. — Common-Size Balance Sheet (20XY Snapshot)

Item	Amount ($)	% of Total Assets
Cash	$10,000	10%
Accounts Receivable	$20,000	20%
Inventory	$30,000	30%
Equipment	$40,000	40%
Total Assets	**$100,000**	**100%**
Accounts Payable	$15,000	15%
Loan	$25,000	25%
Owner's Equity	**$60,000**	**60%**

Quick Practice: Juice Pop Co. Example

Professor FinanceWise smiled. "Before we dive deeper into WoodWorks Co.'s numbers, let's warm up with a quick practice example — a fruit juice stand!"

Sample Common-Size P&L — Juice Pop Co.

Item	Amount ($)	% of Revenue
Revenue	100	100%
Cost of Pineapple	30	30%
Sugar & Cups	20	20%
Net Profit	**50**	**50%**

"This final column (*% of revenue*) is what lets us spot trends, even if the total sales go up or down," said Bella.

The Pricing Problem Revealed

The team met the owner, Mr. Elm, to discuss some concerns about lower pricing that appeared to be affecting revenue.

Mr. Elm: "I made the projections myself... secretly. I didn't want to reveal bids to the team."

Bella: "But that's risky. Even the smartest people can make mistakes."

Final Diagnosis: Fixing Price Mistakes for Smarter Profits

Professor FinanceWise:

"Now we see the real cause — the owner's private price estimates were too low, so WoodWorks undercharged customers. That squeezed profits even though sales looked good."

Bella the Bunny:

"Looks like guessing prices alone can cause big problems!"

Mini-CFO Consulting Report Delivered

Professor FinanceWise:
"To help Mr. Elm remember and share what we found, the Mini-CFO team prepared a simple consulting report. It shows the problems, our recommendations, and next steps — just like real CFO consultants do!"

Bella:
"A report makes sure everyone gets the same story and can take action."

Three Smart Fixes for WoodWorks Co

The team gathered their notes, charts, and calculations and prepared a simple consulting report for Mr. Elm — neatly summarizing the problems they found and the smart fixes he could start using right away.

1. Correct Your Price Targets

Double-check your pricing plans together with your team. Make sure prices cover costs and include healthy profit margins.

2. Build a Team Review Process

Share financial plans openly with trusted people who can help catch mistakes early — don't keep price guesses secret.

3. Track Profits Regularly

Don't wait until year-end. Monitor profit margins each month and compare to targets to spot problems quickly.

Mr. Elm:

"I get it now! I thought I was doing great, but without checks, mistakes hid right under my nose."

Professor FinanceWise:

"Exactly! Smart CFOs don't guess alone — they design processes that help the whole team succeed."

Professor FinanceWise smiled and added, "The Mini-CFO mindset means always asking: Are our prices right? Are our profits what we expected? And how can we improve every day?"

Mini-CFO Wrap-Up: Mystery Solved!

Professor FinanceWise:

"Common-size financials are a powerful lens. They help us compare performance across time — or between businesses of different sizes."

Max:

"Like turning messy numbers into a clean, fair comparison!"

Lily:

"And now we know why WoodWorks Co.'s profit dropped: not because costs increased, but because margins shrank."

Bella:

"That's one more mystery solved!"

The Data Glider took off, and the Mini-CFO Team soared home — mission complete, graphs in hand, and a client one step closer to smarter decisions.

Mini-CFO Consultant Toolbox

Common-Size Income Statement (5-Year Summary)

Item	20XX	20XX	20XX	20XX	20XX
Revenue	100.0%	100.0%	100.0%	100.0%	100.0%
Cost of Goods Sold	40.0%	41.5%	39.8%	42.3%	43.2%
Gross Profit	60.0%	58.5%	60.2%	57.7%	56.8%
Operating Expenses	35.0%	34.0%	32.5%	33.2%	32.0%
Depreciation & Amort.	3.5%	3.2%	2.8%	2.6%	2.5%
Operating Income	21.5%	21.3%	24.9%	21.9%	22.3%
Interest Expense	1.2%	1.0%	1.1%	1.0%	0.8%
Taxes	5.0%	4.9%	5.6%	5.0%	5.2%
Net Income	15.3%	15.4%	18.2%	15.9%	16.3%

Notes:

- **All line items are shown as a percentage of Revenue.**

- **Gross Profit** = Revenue – Cost of Goods Sold

- **Operating Income** = Gross Profit – Operating Expenses – Depreciation

- These percentages help you analyze performance regardless of company size or currency.

Common-Size Balance Sheet (5-Year Summary)

Item	20XX	20XX	20XX	20XX	20XX
Assets					
Cash/Checking/Savings	50.0%	52.5%	55.0%	56.0%	56.8%
Accounts Receivable	30.0%	32.0%	34.0%	34.5%	34.7%
Total Current Assets	80.0%	84.5%	89.0%	90.5%	91.5%
Fixed Assets (Net)	20.0%	15.5%	11.0%	9.5%	8.5%
Total Assets	100.0%	100.0%	100.0%	100.0%	100.0%
Liabilities & Equity					
Accounts Payable	35.0%	34.5%	18.0%	32.0%	31.0%
Total Current Liabilities	35.0%	34.5%	18.0%	32.0%	31.0%
Long-Term Liabilities	10.0%	13.0%	6.5%	3.5%	3.0%
Total Liabilities	45.0%	47.5%	24.5%	35.5%	34.0%
Stockholder's Equity	55.0%	52.5%	75.5%	64.5%	66.0%
Total Liabilities & Equity	100.0%	100.0%	100.0%	100.0%	100.0%

Notes:

- **All asset values are shown as % of Total Assets.**

- **All liabilities and equity are also shown as % of Total Assets** (not of each other).

- Common-size balance sheets help evaluate structural trends like:
  - Working capital changes
  - Reliance on debt vs equity
  - Shifts in asset allocation

Mini-CFO Notes: What These Numbers Really Mean

Professor FinanceWise gave the friends a quick reminder:

"These examples aren't from WoodWorks Co. — they're practice tools. Common-size statements help Mini-CFOs compare any business by turning big numbers into clear percentages. Use them to spot patterns, find problems fast, and see a company's story with clarity."

1. **Revenue is always 100% in common-size statements**
   Everything else is shown as a slice of this 100%.
   That's why comparing different years becomes easy — even if the company grows or shrinks.

2. **Cost of Goods Sold (COGS) shows how efficiently the business produces its products**
   When COGS goes up, it means it costs more to make each item.
   When COGS goes down, efficiency is improving.

3. **Gross Profit reveals the strength of the business model**
   A strong gross profit means the company has room to pay for salaries, marketing, tools, and still make money.

4. **Operating Expenses show how wisely a company manages everyday spending**
   Lower percentages mean the company controls costs well.
   Higher percentages mean the business may be spending too much to operate.

5. **Depreciation tells you how quickly your machines and equipment lose value**
   It's a hidden cost, but CFOs always pay attention because it affects long-term strength.

6. **Operating Income is the Mini-CFO power number**
   It tells you how well the business performs **before** interest or taxes.
   It's the clearest way to compare performance across years.

7. **Net Income shows the final strength of the business**
   It's what remains after all costs, including interest and taxes.

More net income = stronger health.
Less net income = time to investigate and fix.

Mini-CFO Balance Sheet Notes

8. **Assets show where the company's resources live**
   Higher cash percentages mean stronger stability.
   Higher fixed assets mean the company invests in equipment.

9. **Liabilities show obligations**
   A rising liability percentage can be a warning sign — the company might be borrowing too much.

10. **Equity shows the owner's true value in the business**
    Growing equity is a sign of a healthy, winning business.
    Shrinking equity is a sign of trouble.

Why Mini-CFOs Use Common-Size Statements

Because they reveal the truth behind the numbers.
Even if revenue doubles or falls, percentages expose trends that dollars hide:

- Are costs rising faster than sales?

- Are profits shrinking?

- Is the business losing control over expenses?

- Where is efficiency improving?

This is how real CFOs, consultants, and analysts see the company's story — clearly, quickly, and wisely.

Sap Syrup Stand

forest Market

Wooden Spoon Workshop

Ratios REvEal REality

Profit Ratio

Cost Ratio

Debt to Equity

Sales Efficiency

RATiO WHEEL

Resource Ratio

Sap Syrup ⇒ 2 Bottles per Bucket
Spoons Made ⇒ Spoons Sold = 60
Revenue $6,000 ⇒ Profit $1,200 = 20

Revenue $6,000
Profit $1,200
Profit Ratio = 20%

SALES   PROFIT

INPUTS

OUTPUTS

Chapter 13

Ratios — The Mini-CFO's Secret Superpower

It was a bright morning in the forest, and the Mini-CFO team had gathered under the wisdom tree. The sun filtered through the leaves as Professor FinanceWise gently turned his hourglass.

Professor FinanceWise (adjusting his spectacles):

"Mini-CFO team, today I'll show you a magical math trick called a ratio! With this trick, you'll always know how fair, smart, or efficient your money moves are."

What Is a Ratio?

As the team sat cross-legged around the forest stump table, the Professor began explaining.

- A **ratio** compares two numbers so we understand how they relate. Instead of just saying, "We sold 100 pastries", we look at *how many we sold compared to how many we baked*.

- Example: *If we bake 50 pastries and sell 40, the sales ratio is* $\frac{40}{50} = 0.8$ *or* **80%**.

Why Do Ratios Matter?

- Ratios tell us if our business is healthy, efficient, or if we need to improve.

- Ratios let us compare weeks or months — even if totals change!

Professor:
"Big numbers can be confusing. Ratios make sense of them and show us if we're moving toward our goals."

Mini-CFO Examples

Example 1: Sap Syrup Stand

Bella the Bunny:
"We turned 20 buckets of sap into 40 bottles of syrup. That's **2 bottles per bucket!**"

Max the Monkey:

"Last week—10 buckets to 20 bottles—still **2 per bucket**. We're just as efficient!"

Example 2: Wooden Spoon Workshop

Lily:

"We carved 100 spoons but sold just 60. The sales ratio is $\frac{60}{100} = 0.6$ or 60%."

Key Ratios Every Mini-CFO Should Know

Ratio Name	Formula	What It Means
Profit Ratio	$\frac{Profit}{Revenue}$	How much profit we keep per dollar sold
Cost Ratio	$\frac{Cost}{Revenue}$	How much each sale costs us
Sales Efficiency	$\frac{Unit\ Sold}{Units\ Made}$	% of products that found a home
Resource Ratio	$\frac{Input}{Output}$	How much raw material makes each product
Debt-to-Equity	$\frac{Debt}{Owner's\ Capital}$	If we're using borrowed money wisely

Mini-CFO Mystery: The Ratio Reveal

Bella (worried): "We sold more wooden spoons, but our profit dropped! Why?"

Max (checks dashboard): "Our costs have risen faster than our sales."

- **This Month:** Revenue = $6,000, Cost = $4,800, Profit = $1,200, Profit Ratio $= \frac{1200}{6000} = 20\%$

- **Last Month:** Revenue = $5,000, Cost = $3,000, Profit = $2,000, Profit Ratio $= \frac{2000}{5000} = 40\%$

Lily:

"So ratios show us that higher sales don't always mean higher profit!"

Professor FinanceWise (nodding):

"Exactly, Lily. That's the magic of ratios — they reveal truths that big numbers can hide."

Mini-CFO Action Plan

Ratios help you:

- Spot rising costs
- Catch pricing mistakes
- See if you're selling enough vs. production
- Monitor efficiency over time
- **Make smarter choices**

The CFO Lens — Seeing Beyond the Numbers

Professor FinanceWise:

"Mini-CFOs who understand ratios see through noise and into the heart of the business."

Bella:

"So ratios help us catch problems early and make smart decisions?"

Professor:

"Precisely. Numbers tell you what happened. Ratios tell you why it happened — and what to do next."

Reflection Time — What We Learned

Ratios help Mini-CFOs look deeper than totals and discover what's really happening behind the scenes. Whether sales rise, drop, or stay steady, ratios reveal patterns, hidden problems, and opportunities to improve.

Key Takeaway for Kids

Big numbers can be misleading — ratios show the truth. They help you measure fairness, efficiency, and smart decision-making.

Final Inspiration

"Don't just look at numbers. Listen to what they reveal — that's the Mini-CFO superpower."

Trust Is Earned
Through Transparency.

INTERNAL AUDIT
INVESTIGATION BOARD

1 FRAUD PREVENTION
2 FINANCIAL ACCURACY
3 STRONG CONTROLS

WOODCLOCK DEVICES CO

Revenue Error
Inventory Gap
and Cash Leak

Investment Report
Stock Fell from
$150 ⇒ $38 ⇒ $19

Internal
Controls
Checklist

Inventory before
= 40 lemons.
After = 35 sold.
5 missing -
check records!

Cash Inflow: 100 coins
Cash Counted: 95 coins
Where did 5 go?

Cash Drawer

Audit Checklist
Verify,
Record,
Report

- CEOs & CFOs must
ensure strong
internal controls

Chapter 14

The Case of the Disappearing Dollars: How Internal Auditing Protects Businesses

The sun was just beginning to rise over **Prosperity Hollow**, casting golden rays over the town square. Merchants were opening their stalls, bakers kneaded dough, and children ran through the cobbled streets, eager to begin their lessons at the **Hall of Wisdom**.

Inside the Hall, Professor Timeless Wisdom, the wise old owl, adjusted his spectacles and tapped his wooden stand. Timmy the Tortoise, Bella the Bunny, Max the Monkey, and Lily the Ladybug quickly took their seats, excited for today's lesson.

"Today," the Professor began, "we talk about a lesson that can save businesses from ruin and protect hard-earned money—**Internal Auditing.**"

The friends exchanged puzzled looks.

"Internal what?" Max scratched his head.

The Professor smiled. "Let me tell you a story…"

A Costly Mistake – Bella's Mother Learns a Hard Lesson

Bella's ears perked up as the Professor continued.

"A few weeks ago, Bella's mother, Mrs. Hazel, invested her savings—$100,000—in a promising company. The company made fancy clockwork devices and was said to be growing fast! The stock price had been trading at $150 per share, but when the price dropped to $38 per share, Mrs. Hazel saw an opportunity. 'If the price was $150 before, it must go back up!' she thought. So, she bought more shares."

Timmy nodded. "Sounds like a smart plan."

Professor Timeless Wisdom shook his head. "Not always. A few days later, the stock plummeted to $19 per share, and the news broke—the company had weak internal controls and had been manipulating its financial numbers!"

The Professor continued, "A research firm found that the company wasn't following proper accounting rules and had recorded revenue and expenditures incorrectly, not according to US GAAP. The SEC (Securities and Exchange Commission) and Department of Justice started investigating, and the company admitted to financial reporting issues and weak internal controls."

Bella gasped. "Oh no! My mom never told me that part... but I remember she seemed really worried, like something had gone wrong!"

The Professor nodded. "Mrs. Hazel never truly understood what internal auditing meant. But when she invested her hard-earned $100,000 in a promising company—buying shares at $38 each when just days before they were trading at $150—she thought she was making a wise investment. Instead, she watched helplessly as the stock dropped further to $19 amid news of weak internal controls and financial reporting issues.

She learned a hard lesson: internal auditing could have prevented accounts from being manipulated, money from disappearing, and investors from losing confidence—and their savings. From that day on, she became an advocate for strong internal audits and internal controls."

Bella's ears drooped. "If only she had known sooner..."

The Professor gave a wise nod. "And that's why we are learning about this today. A strong internal audit function protects companies, investors, and employees alike."

What Went Wrong?

Lily frowned. "But aren't there auditors in a company who check the numbers?"

The Professor smiled. "Good question! **External auditors check the numbers after they have been recorded. Internal auditors, however, check things before mistakes happen!**"

Timmy adjusted his glasses. "Are those like rules to prevent mistakes?"

"Exactly!" the Professor nodded. **"Think of it like a bakery. If a baker leaves the flour out overnight and doesn't check supplies properly, they might wake up to find rats have eaten the ingredients. A strong internal control would be to lock up the ingredients safely at night."**

Bella's eyes widened. "So, the company my mom invested in didn't lock up its ingredients?"

The Professor nodded. "In a way, yes. **They didn't have strong internal controls to prevent financial misreporting, fraud, and mistakes. When a company lacks good internal auditing, numbers can be manipulated, money can disappear, and investors not only lose confidence but also lose money.**"

Why Internal Controls Matter

Max the Monkey leaned forward. "So, what do these internal auditors do? Are they like detectives?"

The Professor's eyes twinkled. "You're quite right, Max! **Internal auditors are detectives of the business world.** They investigate whether a company is following the right rules and protecting its money. Here are some things they check for:

- **Preventing Fraud** – Making sure no one is stealing or misreporting finances.

- **Financial Accuracy** – Ensuring that the numbers match reality.

- **Risk Management** – Identifying potential issues before they become big problems.

- **Restoring Public Confidence** – Investors trust companies that follow strict auditing rules.

- **Improving Governance** – Making sure businesses operate transparently and ethically.

Lily the Ladybug tapped her tiny notebook. "So, if a company has weak internal controls, it can lose money and get into trouble?"

"Exactly, Lily!" The Professor nodded. "That's why every **CEO (Chief Executive Officer) and CFO (Chief Financial Officer)** must certify that their company has strong internal controls. They are responsible for the **accuracy of financial statements** and ensuring that business operations are **efficient and ethical.**"

A Concern About Internal Auditing

Max looked thoughtful. **"I heard that some CEOs use the internal audit function as a management training ground. Instead of focusing on protecting** the company's financial integrity, internal auditors are moved to other departments to prepare for management roles."

The Professor sighed. "That is true in some companies. Internal auditors with about two years of experience or less, or employees from other departments with similar years of experience, are sometimes hired or transferred into the audit function for a short period to gain exposure to different business functions before moving into management. While this can help future leaders understand company processes and what resources the company has (to effectively utilize them), it can also weaken internal controls if auditing is treated as just a stepping stone rather than a key function for protecting financial integrity. When this happens, investors and stakeholders may face greater risks."

Bella frowned. **"That's bad! If internal auditors don't focus on protecting financial truth, then investors—like my mom—might lose money!"**

The Professor nodded. **"That's why strong internal controls are essential. How internal controls are implemented shows how well a company is governed."**

A Fun Audit Challenge

Max jumped up. "Professor, can we try an audit ourselves?"

The Professor chuckled. "I was hoping you'd ask! I have set up a **mock lemonade stand business** right here in the Hall of Wisdom."

The four friends cheered as they **became internal auditors**, checking for:

- **Cash flow issues** (Did the coins add up correctly?)
- **Supply tracking** (Were lemons missing without explanation?)
- **Proper record-keeping** (Was each sale recorded correctly?)

After completing their audit, they presented their findings and learned **how internal auditors help businesses stay honest and efficient.**

Lessons Learned

As the day ended, the friends reflected on their new knowledge.

Bella: "I understand now why internal controls are so important!"

Max: "Internal auditors are like business detectives, catching problems before they get worse."

Lily: "CEOs and CFOs must make sure companies follow good practices!"

Timmy: "And we, as future Mini-CFOs, must always be responsible with money!"

The Professor smiled. "Well done, my young learners. **Today, you have taken another step on your journey to Mini-CFO Mastery.**"

Reflection Time — What We Learned

Internal auditing protects a company the same way good habits protect a home. When controls are strong and systems are checked regularly, money stays safe, mistakes are caught early, and everyone—from employees to investors—can trust the business.

Key Takeaway for Kids

Strong internal controls keep companies honest, numbers accurate, and investors protected. Before a business can grow, it must guard its money with care and responsibility.

Final Inspiration

"Protect the truth. Strengthen the system. Keep the money safe."

Section 4:

The Strategy and Leadership of CFOs

Theme: *Thinking beyond the numbers — this section develops strategic, managerial, and analytical thinking by introducing children to the mindset of real leaders. Through engaging lessons, young readers explore opportunity cost, competitive advantage, teamwork, long-term planning, and the advanced metrics CFOs use to guide growth.*

Chapter 15

Strategic Resource Allocation & Opportunity Cost

The morning sun sparkled over **Prosperity Hollow**, and the air was filled with the smell of sweet sap syrup. Bella the Bunny, Max the Monkey, Lily the Ladybug, and Timmy the Tortoise hurried to the market square where Professor FinanceWise waited beside a new stall sign that read:

"The Sap Shack: Open for Business!"

"Today," said the Professor, polishing his spectacles, "we learn the secret every Mini-CFO must master — how to choose wisely when you can't do everything at once."

Limited Buckets, Unlimited Dreams

The friends peered at the Sap Shack's supplies.
They had:

- 10 forest coins left in their savings jar,

- 50 empty syrup bottles, and

- A single afternoon to make sales before the Harvest Festival.

Bella smiled. "Let's buy more **sap buckets** so we can make double the syrup!"

Max scratched his head. "Or we could spend the money on **advertising posters** to bring more customers."

Timmy frowned. "But we can't do both… we only have 10 coins."

Professor FinanceWise nodded. "Exactly! You've discovered what every real CFO faces — **limited resources**. Money, time, and energy never stretch forever. Choosing one thing means giving up something else. Every choice has a cost."

Understanding Opportunity Cost

Professor FinanceWise drew two pictures in the dirt:

Option A: Buy 5 more sap buckets → make more syrup
Option B: Print 20 posters → attract more buyers

He asked, "If you choose one, what do you give up?"

Lily flapped her wings. "If we buy buckets, we can't advertise."
"Right," said the Professor. "And if we advertise, we can't buy buckets."

"That's the **opportunity cost** — the value of the next best thing you give up when you make a choice."

He wrote it on his chalkboard:

Opportunity Cost = The next best thing you give up.

"Smart CFOs don't just ask, *'What will I get?'* They also ask, *'What will I lose?'*"

The Test at the Sap Shack

To see the lesson in action, the team decided to test both ideas.

For Day 1, they bought extra sap buckets. They made more syrup but had few customers.

For Day 2, they skipped the buckets and spent coins on colorful posters around the forest. The whole town showed up! They sold out — even with fewer bottles.

Professor FinanceWise smiled:
"So which choice was better?"

"Advertising!" said Bella.
"Because more people knew about us," added Max.
"Exactly," said the Professor. "Sometimes, the *best* use of money isn't the most obvious one. You must think about what gives the **highest return** for each coin or minute you spend."

Mini-CFO Thinking: The Resource Triangle

Professor FinanceWise drew a triangle labeled:

TIME — MONEY — ENERGY

"These are your three main resources," he explained. "Businesses — and people — always balance between them."

- If you spend **more time**, you may save money but feel tired.

- If you spend **more money**, you may save time.

- If you use **too much energy**, you might burn out and lose both time and focus.

"Being a Mini-CFO means deciding how to use each wisely."

Quick Challenge: Which Would You Choose?

Professor FinanceWise gave each student a wooden coin and a question:

1. You can buy **new tools** or **train your team** — what's your opportunity cost?

2. You can spend your afternoon **earning coins** or **learning a new skill** — which builds more value long-term?

3. You can invest in **advertising now** or **save for expansion later** — which grows your business faster?

"Think like a CFO," said the Professor. "There's rarely one right answer — but there's always a smarter reason behind the one you choose."

Wrap-Up Wisdom

As the friends cleaned up the Sap Shack, they counted their coins — and their lessons.

Timmy the Tortoise: "Choosing means losing something."
Bella the Bunny: "But smart choices lose less and gain more!"
Professor FinanceWise nodded. "Exactly. Mini-CFOs plan ahead, compare options, and ask what each choice really costs."

He turned to the class and said:

"Every coin, every hour, every drop of effort has an **opportunity cost**.
Smart CFOs don't just spend — they **strategically allocate**."

Professor's Final Words

"You can do anything — but not everything."
"The best Mini-CFOs think before they spend."

"The cost of a bad choice is not only the coins you lose — it's also the opportunity you miss."

Mini-CFO Action Exercise

Try this at home or in class:

1. List **two things** you want to do this week.

2. Write down what each one costs (time or money).

3. Circle which one helps your **future goals** more.

4. That's your best resource allocation — your Mini-CFO move!

Reflection Time — What We Learned

Every choice we make uses time, money, or energy — and each choice has a cost. When we understand what we gain *and* what we give up, we make wiser decisions and use our resources more powerfully.

Key Takeaway for Kids

Opportunity cost isn't about losing something — it's about choosing the option that builds your future the most. Smart Mini-CFOs pick what creates the greatest value.

Final Inspiration

"Choose with clarity. Invest with intention. Let your decisions build your future."

Winner: The Sap Syrup Stand
— For Innovation, Quality & Story!

HONEY HUT

SWEET SAP FOR SALE!
Gathered by Friends
— Shared with Heart.

MINI-CFO
ADVANTAGE FORMULA:
QUALITY · SPEED · PRICE
UNIQUENESS · STORY

Speed Team

Made fresh from
first-drop forest sap
— no sugar added

Chapter 16

Building Competitive Advantage

The morning buzz in **Prosperity Hollow** was louder than ever. Two new stands had opened side by side in the town square:

The Sap Syrup Stand — run by the four young entrepreneurs, and
Honey Hut — a shiny new stall with golden jars and a cheerful bee mascot.

The crowd gathered, curious to try both.

Bella whispered nervously, "They're selling sweet syrup too!"
Max frowned. "And they have jingles! We need one of those!"
Timmy adjusted his glasses. "Professor FinanceWise, how do we compete with that?"

The Professor smiled. "Ah, my young Mini-CFOs, you've just met your next great lesson — *competitive advantage!*"

What Is Competition — and Why Does It Matter?

Professor FinanceWise perched on a wooden crate.
"In every marketplace — from lemonade stands to global companies — others will offer similar products. Competition keeps everyone improving."

He drew two trees on his chalkboard: one tall and strong, the other smaller but growing fast.
"The strong tree stands tall because it found better sunlight and stronger roots. That's what a business does when it builds **competitive advantage** — it finds its sunlight before others do."

"Without it," said Lily, "everyone just copies each other."

"Exactly!" said the Professor. "When products are the same, customers choose whoever is cheaper — and soon, no one wins. But when you offer something *different*, something *better*, customers choose you for your value — not just your price."

The Great Prosperity Hollow Taste Test

The next morning, the Mayor announced a festival challenge:

"The Sweet Success Contest — best syrup in town wins a golden spoon!"

Both the Sap Syrup Stand and Honey Hut would compete.

The friends gathered for a strategy meeting.

Bella: "Honey Hut's jars look fancy."
Max: "Their bee costume is drawing crowds."
Timmy: "But our syrup tastes richer!"
Lily: "We need to prove that!"

Professor FinanceWise nodded. "Let's use the Mini-CFO Advantage Framework."

He wrote five golden words on the board:

Quality – Speed – Price – Uniqueness – Story

"These," he said, "are the five ways a Mini-CFO can help a business stand out."

1. Compete on Quality

Bella dipped a wooden spoon into their syrup. "We already use the finest sap and natural herbs."

"Then show it!" said the Professor.
They printed small cards:
"Made fresh from first-drop forest sap — no sugar added!"

"Customers trust transparency," the Professor said.
"When you prove quality, you earn loyalty — and loyal customers beat discounts every time."

2. Compete on Speed

Max waved his tail. "We can serve faster if we organize better!"
He rearranged their stand — one person poured, one sealed bottles, one handled coins.

"Efficiency is an advantage too," said the Professor.
"Customers value time. Faster service feels like better service."

3. Compete on Price — But Smartly

Timmy studied the numbers. "If we lower prices too much, profits shrink."

"Correct," said the Professor. "Low prices can attract crowds, but only if your **cost structure** supports it."

He explained with a small table:

Strategy	Example	CFO Thinking
Low-Cost Advantage	Sell more bottles at smaller profit each	Must control costs tightly
Premium Advantage	Higher price, higher quality	Must deliver real value
Balanced Strategy	Reasonable price, reliable quality	Builds long-term trust

"Price," said the Professor, "is a reflection of strategy — not a random number."

4. Compete on Uniqueness

Lily, the creative spark, fluttered her wings. "What if we add a new flavor — sap-cinnamon swirl?"

"Brilliant!" said the Professor. "Innovation is one of the most powerful advantages. It gives customers a reason to come back."

Soon, the sweet scent of sap-cinnamon syrup filled the air. The line at their stand doubled.

5. Compete on Story

Professor FinanceWise gestured toward their hand-painted banner:

"Gathered by Friends — Shared with Heart"

"That," he said, "is your story. People buy not only products, but purpose. When your story connects to meaning — teamwork, honesty, community — you win hearts, not just wallets."

Bella smiled. "Honey Hut has honey. We have heart."

The Golden Spoon Results

When the Mayor announced the winner, the town erupted in applause —
The Sap Syrup Stand had won!

Their syrup wasn't just delicious — it told a story, was served faster, and
showed integrity in every drop.

Professor FinanceWise raised his wing:
"See? You didn't try to be the cheapest. You built *value*. That's the heart of
competitive advantage — making people choose you for what you do best."

Mini-CFO Deep Dive: Strategy Behind the Scenes

Later, under the Wisdom Tree, the Professor shared how CFOs strengthen
advantage behind the curtain:

1. **Invest in Better Tools**
   → "Use profits to buy sap filters and temperature sensors — consistency
   builds reputation."

2. **Use Data for Decisions**
   → "Track which flavor sells best and adjust inventory — that's financial
   intelligence."

3. **Build Team Skills**
   → "A trained team produces quality faster — every hour saved adds profit."

4. **Plan for the Future**
   → "If competition copies you, what's next? Innovation is a cycle, not a one-
   time win."

5. **Protect Your Edge**
   → "Keep recipes, designs, and processes documented — your unique
   advantage is a valuable asset."

The Mini-CFO Advantage Formula

Competitive Advantage = (Unique Value + Efficient Systems + Smart Pricing + Strong Story)

Mini-CFOs don't chase crowds — they **create clarity**.
They study what customers truly value, invest in the right places, and ensure every coin spent strengthens the business's position.

Professor's Final Words

"The biggest risk is blending in."
"Profit follows purpose — not panic."
"A true CFO doesn't just count coins; they build *moats* that protect the castle."

Mini-CFO Activity: Build Your Advantage Map

Draw your own small business idea — maybe a cookie stand, art shop, or pet-care service.
Then fill in these boxes:

Area	My Advantage	How I'll Keep It Strong
Quality	_____	_____
Speed	_____	_____
Price	_____	_____
Uniqueness	_____	_____
Story	_____	_____

Professor's Challenge:
"Explain your strongest advantage to someone — if they remember it easily, your business is already standing strong."

Reflection Time — What We Learned

Competitive advantage is what makes a business stand out in a crowded marketplace. Whether it's quality, speed, pricing, uniqueness, or a meaningful story, every strong business chooses a special way to shine — and protects it with smart decisions.

Key Takeaway for Kids

Winning isn't about being the cheapest or the loudest — it's about offering something special that customers remember and trust. Your unique strengths are your greatest advantage.

Final Inspiration

"Stand out with purpose. Strengthen your edge. Let your value shine."

Chapter 17

Financial Leadership & Team Management

T he wind danced gently through the Hall of Wisdom as the golden bell chimed.

Professor FinanceWise stood at the podium with a calm smile.
"Mini-CFOs," he said, "today we step into the most powerful lesson of all — how to lead."

Bella the Bunny looked puzzled.
"But Professor, CFOs work with money, not people — right?"

Professor FinanceWise chuckled.
"Oh, Bella! Numbers tell a story, but people make that story happen.
A true CFO doesn't just manage money — they **lead people** to make wise choices with it."

The River Project: When Numbers Meet People

Prosperity Hollow was planning a new bridge across the Crystal River.
The Mayor asked the Hall of Wisdom to help manage the project's coins and plans.

The Professor turned to the Mini-CFO team.
"Friends, this project will test both your math and your management."

Each friend took a role:

- **Timmy the Tortoise**: Record-keeper and budget tracker

- **Bella the Bunny**: Procurement — finding fair prices for wood and stone

- **Max the Monkey**: Operations — making sure work stayed on schedule

- **Lily the Ladybug**: Communications — sharing updates with the town

At first, everything went smoothly. But after two weeks, things began to wobble.

Max complained, "The workers keep running out of tools!"
Bella frowned, "Because Timmy's budget releases coins too slowly!"
Timmy defended, "I'm just being careful with spending!"
Lily sighed, "And the townspeople are getting restless for updates."

The Professor watched quietly, then said,
"It seems we've hit a leadership test."

Lesson 1: Leadership Starts With Listening

The Professor gathered the team under the big oak tree.
"Before you lead, you must listen," he said.

He handed each of them a small brass key engraved with one word — **Empathy**.

"Listening doesn't mean agreeing with everyone," said the Professor.
"It means understanding how each person sees the problem — and finding a shared path forward."

They began listening to one another.

Timmy learned that the workers needed tools faster.
Bella realized her price checks took too long.
Max understood why patience mattered.
Lily found better ways to explain the project's progress to the town.

Soon, everyone felt heard — and teamwork began to flow again.

Lesson 2: The CFO Leads With Clarity

Professor FinanceWise spread a large parchment scroll across the table — a financial dashboard.

"A CFO's greatest tool," he said, "is *clarity*. When people see the full picture, they make better choices."

He drew three columns:

Team	Task	Budget Coins
Builders	Bridge frame	50
Painters	Finish & seal	20
Safety Team	Rails & testing	30

Then he added one more column: **Status – On Track / Behind / Ahead**

"Transparency builds trust," said the Professor. "When you show your plan openly, others see you as fair and reliable — that's real leadership."

Lesson 3: Delegation and Trust

One morning, Max tried to do everything himself.
He bought wood, managed workers, even tried to count the coins.
By noon, he was exhausted — and mistakes piled up.

Professor FinanceWise approached gently.
"Max, even the strongest leader cannot carry every bucket."

He handed Max a feather-light compass.

"This compass points to trust," he said. "When you trust your team and delegate wisely, everyone grows."

Max nodded. He gave Bella control of purchases, Timmy oversight of funds, and Lily the task of sharing progress.
Within days, efficiency soared — and the bridge began to take shape.

Lesson 4: Honest Reporting — Even When It's Hard

Halfway through construction, Timmy discovered they had spent more coins than planned.
Nervous, he whispered to the Professor, "Should I tell the others? They'll be upset."

Professor FinanceWise's eyes twinkled.
"Honesty may sting for a moment — but dishonesty wounds forever.
Financial leaders earn trust not by being perfect, but by being **truthful**."

Timmy gathered the team.
"I made a mistake in estimating. We're over budget by 10 coins."

Instead of anger, the friends nodded.
Bella said, "Good catch — now we can fix it."
Lily added, "Let's explain it clearly to the Mayor. Transparency shows maturity."

That day, Timmy learned that **integrity is a CFO's invisible armor.**

Lesson 5: From Boss to Builder — The Heart of Team Management

Professor FinanceWise gathered everyone on the new bridge as the sun set over the water.

"Do you see this?" he said, pointing to the reflection below.
"This bridge stands because you worked as a team. Each coin was a decision, but each decision was built on trust."

He turned to them with pride.
"Leadership is not about shouting orders or holding the biggest calculator. It's about inspiring others, solving problems together, and keeping your team calm when numbers get tough."

Mini-CFO Leadership Code

Value	What It Means	Example
Integrity	Always tell the truth about numbers	Admit errors and fix them fast
Clarity	Share goals and progress openly	Use dashboards or charts
Empathy	Understand your team's challenges	Listen before deciding
Accountability	Take responsibility for outcomes	Don't blame others
Vision	Connect daily work to long-term goals	Remind the team *why* it matters

Professor's Final Words

"Leadership isn't a title — it's a responsibility."
"A CFO who wins trust can guide thousands of coins and countless hearts."
"Numbers tell what happened; people make it happen."

He smiled as the friends admired their finished bridge.

"Remember, Mini-CFOs, leadership and teamwork aren't just soft skills —
they're strategic assets.
A great CFO turns numbers into stories, and teams into success."

Mini-CFO Activity: Build Your Leadership Ledger

Draw two columns in your notebook:

Left Column: "What Makes a Good Leader"
Right Column: "How I Can Practice It This Week"

Example:

- Listen first before deciding.

- Keep track of chores with honesty.

- Thank teammates when they help.

Professor's Challenge:
"Leadership starts now — not when you grow up.
Practice today, and someday, you'll lead both people *and* prosperity."

Reflection Time — What We Learned

Leadership is more than guiding numbers — it is guiding people. When we
listen, communicate clearly, share responsibility, and remain honest even in
difficult moments, we turn challenges into teamwork and teamwork into success.

Key Takeaway for Kids

A great leader is not the loudest or the fastest — but the one who helps others
do their best. True financial leadership starts with empathy, clarity, trust, and
responsibility.

Final Inspiration

"Lead with integrity, listen with heart, and let your actions inspire your team."

Innovation,
People,
Resilience,
Vision.

Future Plans

Mini-CFO Growth Dashboard

Reinvest
Improve
Grow
People
Legacy

Growth Cycle
Profit →
Reinvest →
Improve →
Grow →
→ Repeat

Chapter 18

Long-Term Planning & Growth Strategy

T he town of **Prosperity Hollow** shimmered in the soft glow of evening. The marketplace was winding down, and the sweet smell of sap syrup and wood polish filled the air.

Professor FinanceWise gathered his four young apprentices beneath the Great Oak, holding a candle lantern that flickered like a tiny sun.

"Mini-CFOs," he said, "we've learned to earn, save, spend, and lead. Now it's time for your next great superpower — *thinking beyond today*."

The Lesson of the WoodWorks Co.

"Remember our friends at WoodWorks Co.?" asked the Professor.
"They make fine tables, chairs, and wooden toys — and business is booming again."

Bella the Bunny nodded. "They fixed their profit problems after our consulting visit!"

"Indeed," said the Professor. "But now they face a new challenge — deciding what to do with their profit."

He unrolled a scroll showing two paths:

Path A: Spend the profits now — bigger bonuses, new signs, fancy office.
Path B: Reinvest part of the profits — buy better tools, train workers, plant more trees for future wood.

Max the Monkey raised a hand. "Spending sounds fun — but reinvesting builds more, right?"

Professor FinanceWise smiled. "Exactly. Short-term fun often fades. Long-term growth creates legacy."

Lesson 1: What Is Long-Term Planning?

The Professor drew a winding road across the chalkboard.

"Short-term thinking is about *today's coins*.
Long-term thinking is about *tomorrow's forests*."

He wrote:

Short-Term → What do we gain today?
Long-Term → What do we build for tomorrow?

He explained, "When a Mini-CFO plans long-term, they imagine where their business could be in one year, five years, even ten. They make small choices today that open big doors tomorrow."

Lesson 2: The Power of Reinvestment

The next morning, the team visited WoodWorks Co.
The owner, Mr. Elm, showed them two piles of coins.

"One pile is for bonuses. The other, I'm thinking of saving for better cutting tools," he said. "But my workers want their rewards now."

Professor FinanceWise replied, "Rewarding your team is good — but so is preparing for their future. What if next year you could pay them *double* because your tools made production faster?"

The Professor turned to the Mini-CFO team.
"Who remembers the formula for growth?"

Lily fluttered her wings. "Invest → Improve → Earn → Reinvest → Grow!"

"Perfect!" said the Professor. "That's the **Cycle of Sustainable Growth.**"

He drew it on the board:

Profit → Reinvest → Improve → Grow → Repeat

Timmy the Tortoise smiled slowly. "So it's like planting seeds instead of eating them all."

Mini-CFO Story: The Baker's Big Vision

Professor FinanceWise told a tale from the neighboring village.

There once was a baker who earned ten coins a day.
Each evening, she had two choices — spend all her coins on sweets, or save a few to buy better ovens.

The baker chose patience.

Every month she bought one small upgrade — a better whisk, a faster mixer, a bigger oven.

Soon, her bakery grew so efficient that she served three towns instead of one.

"Her patience was her profit multiplier," said the Professor. "That's long-term strategy in action."

Lesson 3: CFO Tools for Future Growth

Professor FinanceWise set out three golden scrolls on the table.

Scroll 1: Forecasting

"Use numbers from today to estimate tomorrow. If we sold 100 jars this month and expect 10% more customers next month, we can forecast 110 jars.
That helps us prepare for materials, workers, and savings."

Scroll 2: Scenario Planning

"Ask 'What if?' questions.
What if sales drop? What if costs rise? What if a new shop opens?
CFOs create multiple plans so the future doesn't surprise them."

Scroll 3: Compounding Growth

"Small steady growth adds up.
A business that grows 10% a year doubles in about seven years — that's the magic of compounding growth.
That's the power of patience and consistency."

Lesson 4: Vision — Seeing What Others Don't

The friends gathered by the river bridge they'd helped build.

Professor FinanceWise said, "When others see a bridge, a CFO sees a *pathway* — to trade, tourism, and opportunity."

He gave each of them a small crystal labeled **Vision**.

"A Mini-CFO doesn't just look at what *is* — they imagine what *could be*.
That's how big companies grow from small stands. They dream with direction."

Lesson 5: Planning for People, Not Just Profits

Bella asked, "But what if people get tired waiting for rewards?"

"Ah," said the Professor, "a wise CFO grows people along with profits."

He explained:
"When you plan for growth, also plan for your team — training, better tools, fair rewards.
Growth that forgets people will eventually stop growing."

Lily nodded. "So sustainable growth means the business, people, and community all rise together!"

"Exactly," said the Professor. "That's what true leadership looks like."

The WoodWorks Decision

The next week, WoodWorks Co. presented its new plan:

- 60% of profit → shared with workers as rewards

- 30% → reinvested in new carving tools

- 10% → planted a new row of young trees

A year later, their profits doubled — and their forests grew too.

"See?" said Professor FinanceWise. "They didn't chase growth. They *built* it."

Mini-CFO Growth Dashboard

Growth Area	Example Action	Long-Term Impact
Product Quality	Buy better tools or materials	Fewer returns, stronger reputation
Efficiency	Train team in time-saving methods	More production with same effort
Innovation	Create a new design or flavor	Stand out from competition

Growth Area	Example Action	Long-Term Impact
People	Share profits, invest in learning	Happier, loyal team
Resilience	Save a portion each year	Safety during hard times

Professor's Final Words

"A coin spent can bring joy. A coin reinvested can build a future."
"Growth is not luck — it's strategy, patience, and purpose."
"A great CFO doesn't predict the future — they *prepare* for it."

He looked toward the horizon, where the sun met the forest line.

"Mini-CFOs, never stop asking: *What can I do today to make tomorrow stronger?*
Because planning for the future isn't just about profit — it's about *possibility*."

Mini-CFO Activity: Plant Your Future Tree

Draw a tree on your journal.
Label the trunk **"Today's Effort."**
Then write your future dreams as branches — things you want to build, learn, or grow.
Next to each branch, note what small habit or action today will feed that growth.

Professor's Challenge:
"Visit your tree each month. Add new leaves as your ideas — and your wisdom — grow."

Reflection Time — What We Learned

Long-term success is built one wise choice at a time. When we reinvest, plan ahead, imagine future possibilities, and stay patient, small actions today become big achievements tomorrow. True growth comes from thinking beyond the moment and preparing for the future with purpose.

Key Takeaway for Kids

Big dreams grow from small, steady steps. Reinvesting your effort, planning carefully, and staying consistent turns today's seeds into tomorrow's forests.

Final Inspiration

"Plant wisely, plan boldly, and let your future grow strong."

Chapter 19

Advanced Financial Metrics & KPIs

The morning sun streamed through the tall windows of the **Hall of Wisdom**, casting golden rectangles on the floor. The four friends — Bella the Bunny, Timmy the Tortoise, Max the Monkey, and Lily the Ladybug — sat around a large wooden table stacked with charts, scrolls, and syrup bottles.

Professor FinanceWise walked in carrying a small glass compass that glowed faintly with numbers.

"Good morning, Mini-CFOs," he said with a smile. "Today, we won't just talk about making money — we'll learn how to **measure success** the way real CFOs do."

Lesson 1: More Than Just Profits

Bella tilted her head. "But Professor, isn't profit the whole point?"

Professor FinanceWise chuckled.
"Ah, Bella — profit is important, but it's only one part of the story. A wise CFO looks beyond the number at the bottom of the page."

He drew three circles on the chalkboard and labeled them:

Profit, **Performance**, and **People**.

"**Profit** tells us what we earned.
Performance shows how well we used our resources.
People reflect how happy our customers and team are.

Great businesses balance all three."

Lesson 2: What Is a KPI?

Lily fluttered her tiny wings. "Professor, what's a KPI?"

"A KPI," said the Professor, "means **Key Performance Indicator** — a special number that helps you track how your business is doing."

He tapped the compass in his hand.
"This compass doesn't point north — it points toward *progress.*

Each KPI is like a little arrow showing whether you're moving closer to your goal or drifting away."

He wrote on the board:

KPIs = Clues that tell you what's working and what needs fixing.

Lesson 3: Simple KPIs for Mini-CFOs

The Professor opened a scroll titled *"The Prosperity Hollow Dashboard."*
Inside were colorful charts, each with a smiling or frowning face.

KPI Name	What It Means	Example
Cash Flow	Money coming in vs. going out	"Do we have enough to pay for lemons next week?"
Break-Even Point	When sales cover all costs	"How many jars must we sell before we start earning profit?"
Sales Growth	How much sales increased compared to last month	"Did we sell more or less syrup than before?"
Customer Happiness Score	How much customers love your product	"Would they buy again or tell friends?"
Inventory Turnover	How quickly stock sells	"Are bottles sitting too long on the shelf?"

"Each of these," said the Professor, "is a lens that helps you see clearly — and see ahead."

Lesson 4: The Case of the Dropping Happiness Scores

One morning, Max burst into the Hall of Wisdom waving a parchment.
"Professor! Our syrup sales are up 20%, but our *Happy Customer Scores* fell from 9 to 7!"

Bella looked shocked. "But higher sales mean success, right?"

Professor FinanceWise frowned gently. "Not if our customers are growing unhappy.

Let's find out *why*."

The team went to the market and spoke to customers.
Some said the syrup was delicious but the lines were long.
Others loved the taste but missed their favorite cinnamon flavor.

Timmy recorded every comment in the **Mini-CFO Feedback Ledger.**

Back at the Hall, the Professor said,
"This is why KPIs are powerful — they reveal problems before they become disasters. Sales growth looks great, but falling happiness could warn of trouble ahead."

Lesson 5: Turning Data into Decisions

Bella flipped open her notebook. "So what should we do?"

Professor FinanceWise smiled. "Mini-CFOs don't guess — they act on data."

They reviewed each KPI:

- **Cash Flow:** Still healthy.

- **Inventory Turnover:** Slowing down — too many bottles waiting.

- **Happiness Score:** Dropping.

- **Sales Growth:** Up — but flattening after the first week.

Lily concluded, "Maybe we're producing too much of the wrong flavor!"
The Professor nodded. "Exactly. Let's adjust production toward what customers love most."

The next week, they reintroduced the cinnamon-swirl syrup and improved service speed.
Their Happiness Score jumped back to **9.5**, and sales grew even higher.

Lesson 6: CFO Thinking — Metrics as a Map

Professor FinanceWise spread out a parchment map of Prosperity Hollow. "KPIs are like signposts on a journey," he said. "If one arrow points off course, you don't panic — you **adjust.**"

He pointed to different spots on the map:

- "Cash Flow" kept their business alive day by day.

- "Sales Growth" told them if they were expanding.

- "Customer Happiness" kept their reputation shining.

- "Efficiency Ratios" made sure they weren't wasting effort.

"When you track the right numbers, you make the right decisions," said the Professor. "That's the true art of financial leadership."

Mini-CFO Dashboard: Build Your Own

KPI	Target	Actual	Result
Cash Flow	Positive	✓	Healthy
Sales Growth	+10% per month	+12%	Great!
Customer Happiness	9/10	9.5/10	Excellent
Inventory Turnover	100% in 2 weeks	3 weeks	Needs improvement
Profit Margin	25%	27%	Slightly ahead

Professor FinanceWise smiled.
"When you can *see* your numbers like this, you don't wait for problems — you solve them early. That's what CFOs do every day."

Lesson 7: The Secret Ingredient — Balance

Timmy raised his hand. "But, Professor, that's a lot of numbers! Which one matters most?"

"Ah," said the Professor, "a very wise question. The answer is balance.
If you only chase sales, you might ignore cash.
If you only watch cash, you might forget customers.
KPIs must work together — like a team."

He tapped the compass again.
"Remember: A compass doesn't show one direction; it shows balance among all sides."

Professor's Final Words

"KPIs are not just numbers — they are *stories* told by data."
"Measure what matters, not just what's easy."
"Great CFOs listen to their numbers the way captains listen to the wind — constantly adjusting the sails."

The Professor looked at the Mini-CFO team and smiled.
"Today, you've learned how real leaders make decisions — not by luck, but by **listening to the language of numbers.**"

Mini-CFO Activity: Create Your Business Dashboard

1. Choose a small project (lemonade stand, art sale, or school fundraiser).

2. Pick **3–5 KPIs** you'll track (e.g., savings rate, sales, customer smiles, or time efficiency).

3. Draw your **dashboard** with color bars or faces to show progress each week.

4. Ask: "Which area improved? Which needs help?"

5. Adjust your actions — and celebrate the results!

Professor's Challenge:

"Don't fear your numbers — make friends with them.
Because every smart decision begins with what you *measure*."

Reflection Time — What We Learned

KPIs turn numbers into insights. They help businesses understand what's working, what's slipping, and what needs attention before problems grow. When Mini-CFOs listen closely to their data, they make decisions that keep customers happy, improve performance, and strengthen long-term success.

Key Takeaway for Kids

Numbers are more than math — they're signals. By tracking the right KPIs and paying attention to trends, you can guide any project or business in the right direction.

Final Inspiration

"Measure wisely, adjust boldly, and let your numbers guide your next great step."

Section 5:

The Heart of a True CFO

Theme: *Integrity, vision, and ethics are the true hallmarks of great financial leaders. This section guides children to understand why honesty, fairness, transparency, and responsible decision-making shape the character of a Mini-CFO. It invites young readers to reflect, grow, and embrace the values that strengthen both leadership and life.*

THE PILLARS OF TRUST

HONESTY   FAIRNESS   TRANSPAREN

Integrity =
Protecting Truth
Under Pressure.

THE PILLARS OF TRUST

HONESTY

TRANSPARENCY   FAIRNESS

TRANSPARENCY
REPORT

ETHICAL
ACTION
PLAN

Honesty: Admit mistakes → earn trust
Fairness: Treat everyone right → build loyalty
Transparency : Show truth → inspire confidence

Chapter 20

Mini-CFO Ethics — Honesty, Fairness, and Transparency

The candles flickered in the **Hall of Wisdom** as the Mini-CFO team gathered one last time.

Professor FinanceWise perched on his wooden stand, feathers shining in the golden glow.

"Mini-CFOs," he began softly, "we've talked about money, growth, and strategy.

But there's a superpower even stronger than all of those."

Bella the Bunny leaned forward. "Stronger than profit?"
"Much stronger," said the Professor.
"It's called **Ethics** — the courage to do what's right, even when it's hard."

Lesson 1: Why Ethics Matters

The Professor drew a triangle on the board and labeled its corners:

Honesty – Fairness – Transparency

"These three pillars hold up every trustworthy business," he explained.
"If one breaks, the whole structure wobbles — even if the profits look high."

Max the Monkey tilted his head. "But Professor, can't a business still make money if it's not honest?"

The Professor sighed. "For a short time, perhaps. But dishonesty is like a leak in a boat.
You may float for a while, but eventually — you sink."

Lesson 2: Honesty — The Foundation of Trust

The Professor began a story.
"In Prosperity Hollow, there once was a merchant named **Mr. Oakleaf**, who sold flour and grain.
One day he noticed his scale was slightly off — customers paid for a full bag, but got a little less."

Bella gasped. "Did he fix it?"

"At first, he thought, *'No one will notice — it's just a little mistake.'* But his conscience felt heavy.
So he told his customers, replaced the bags, and repaired the scale."

"What happened then?" asked Lily.

"Word spread quickly — not about his mistake, but about his **honesty**.
People began trusting him more than ever, and his shop grew busier than before."

The Professor turned to Max.
"See, Max — honesty might cost a few coins today, but it earns trust that lasts a lifetime.
A true CFO never hides mistakes — they **face them, fix them, and learn from them.**"

Lesson 3: Fairness — Treating Everyone Right

The next day, the friends visited the forest fair.
Two food stalls sold berry pies — one offered discounts only to rich travelers; the other treated everyone equally.

"Which stall do you think earned more loyal customers?" asked the Professor.
"The fair one!" said Bella.

"Correct. Fairness builds reputation, and reputation is a **strategic asset.**
CFOs protect fairness not only in prices, but in pay, opportunities, and partnerships."

Timmy the Tortoise added thoughtfully,
"So fairness isn't just being kind — it's smart business too."

"Exactly," said the Professor. "When your team feels respected, they work harder.
When your customers feel valued, they return.
Fairness is the quiet engine that powers long-term success."

Lesson 4: Transparency — Sharing the Real Story

Back in the Hall, Professor FinanceWise unrolled a parchment filled with colorful charts.
"These," he said, "are our latest financial results."

The friends leaned in eagerly.
Lily pointed to a red line. "That looks bad!"
"Yes," said the Professor. "It means our costs rose last month. But hiding it would only make it worse."

He wrote on the board:

Transparency = Sharing the real story, even when it's uncomfortable.

"Good CFOs show facts clearly. Great CFOs help others understand them. Transparency builds confidence — among customers, workers, even investors."

Max asked, "But what if being transparent makes people upset?"
"Then you explain the *why* behind the numbers," replied the Professor.
"People forgive problems; they don't forgive secrecy."

Lesson 5: The Real-World Test — Pressure at the Top

The Professor's tone turned serious.
"Even big CFOs face temptation. Sometimes CEOs or board members want numbers to 'look better' —
to impress investors or win bonuses."

Bella's eyes widened. "So… what should a CFO do?"

The Professor looked around the room.
"A courageous CFO speaks the truth — respectfully, but firmly.
They remember their duty is not to please people, but to **protect integrity**."

Professor FinanceWise looked around the room and said gravely,
"In real companies, CFOs must sign and **attest that financial reports and internal controls are accurate.**

If they manipulate numbers, they can be **caught by regulators like the SEC (Securities and Exchange Commission)**, and lose not only their jobs — but their reputation and the public's trust."

He drew a small shield on the board labeled:

Integrity = Protecting truth even under pressure.

"Numbers can be changed. Character cannot.
A CFO's real job is not just counting coins — it's guarding the trust that keeps the business alive."

Lily whispered, "That must be scary sometimes."
The Professor nodded. "It is. But courage grows with practice — just like leadership."

Lesson 6: Ethics as a Strategic Superpower

The Professor gestured to three golden scrolls.

Scroll 1: Honesty Protects the Future
→ "When people trust your numbers, you attract investors, partners, and loyal customers."

Scroll 2: Fairness Strengthens Teams
→ "A fair workplace keeps employees motivated and creative — that's productivity in disguise."

Scroll 3: Transparency Prevents Trouble
→ "Clear records and open reports stop problems before they grow."

He turned to the team.
"You see, ethics isn't just about goodness — it's about **good governance.**
When you lead with integrity, you reduce risk, avoid costly scandals, and keep your reputation shining.
That's the smartest strategy any CFO can follow."

Mini-CFO Story: The Festival Donation

During the Harvest Festival, the Mayor asked all businesses to donate a share of their profits to rebuild the community hall.
The Mini-CFO team met to decide how much.

Max wanted to keep most of their earnings for expansion.
Bella thought they should give generously.
Timmy said, "Let's be fair — balance our needs and the town's."

Professor FinanceWise smiled. "Well said, Timmy. Ethics often means **balance** — doing what's right for everyone, not just ourselves."

They donated a fair share, and their act of integrity brought new respect — and even more customers.

Mini-CFO Ethical Action Plan

Principle	Example	Why It Matters
Honesty	Admit mistakes quickly and correct them	Builds long-term trust
Fairness	Offer equal treatment and fair prices	Keeps customers and teams loyal
Transparency	Share clear reports and progress	Prevents misunderstandings
Courage	Speak up when pressured to "adjust" the truth	Protects reputation and conscience

Professor's Final Words

"Numbers tell stories — ethics makes those stories worth believing."
"When you protect truth, you protect value."
"The best CFOs lead not just with brains, but with backbone."

He looked at his young students proudly.

"Mini-CFOs, someday you'll manage great organizations, budgets, or maybe even nations.

Remember this: **profits build companies, but ethics builds legacies.**"

As the candles dimmed and the Hall grew quiet, Professor FinanceWise whispered one last thought:

"In the world of finance, your reputation is your most valuable asset. Guard it like gold — and you'll shine for a lifetime."

Mini-CFO Activity: The Ethics Test

Try this each week:

1. **Spot a Dilemma:** Notice when you face a choice between "easy" and "right."

2. **Ask:** What would build trust if others knew about my choice?

3. **Act:** Choose honesty, fairness, and transparency — even if it's hard.

4. **Reflect:** How did that choice make you feel stronger inside?

Professor's Challenge:

"When no one is watching, choose what you'd be proud to explain. That's the moment you become a true CFO — and a true leader."

Reflection Time — What We Learned

Ethics is the silent force that shapes every business. Honesty builds trust, fairness builds loyalty, and transparency builds confidence. When we protect the truth — even in tough moments — we strengthen both our character and our future.

Key Takeaway for Kids

Being a great Mini-CFO isn't just about counting coins — it's about choosing what's right. Integrity turns small decisions into lifelong strength.

Final Inspiration

"Do what's right, even when it's hard — that's how leaders shine."

Author's Note

Dear Reader,

Congratulations — you've reached the end of *Mini-CFO Adventures!*
You've explored the heart of Prosperity Hollow, learned from Professor FinanceWise, and discovered what it truly means to *think like a Chief Financial Officer* — someone who leads with **clarity, courage, and character**.

This book is a little different from most stories about money.
It's designed to help young readers build not just financial knowledge, but **strategic financial thinking** — the kind of mindset real CFOs use to make thoughtful decisions, plan for growth, and lead with integrity.

Because understanding money is important — but **understanding how to think** about money is what creates real wisdom.

When you plan your allowance, run a small stand, or save for a dream, you're already practicing the same habits that guide real companies:
setting goals, managing resources, and thinking ahead.
And when you choose honesty over shortcuts, you're building something even more powerful — *trust*, the foundation of all great leadership.

Keep your curiosity alive. Keep asking "why."
Use what you learned here to help others, lead projects, and grow into a thinker who makes both good profits and good decisions.

You are now a **Mini-Finance Strategist** — someone who understands that money is not the goal, but a tool for creating opportunity, stability, and impact.

I'm proud of the wisdom you've gained and even more excited for the journeys ahead.

The world needs leaders like you — leaders who use numbers to build trust, strategy, and hope.

— **Dr. Joy Chacko, PhD**
CFO Strategist & Author of the Skillful Adventures™ Series

Quick Reflection

- What financial lesson surprised me the most?

- How can I use what I learned to make better choices this week?

- Who helped me grow during this adventure?

- What does being a "Mini-CFO" mean to me now?

☀ Bonus Resources

Visit **SkillfulAdventures.com** for free toolkits, checklists, and planners — designed for kids, parents, and teachers who want to instill strong skills early and keep growing in the language of leadership, finance, and strategy.

References &
Reflection Tools

Glossary — Mini-CFO Words You Should Know 🔍

Accountability – Taking responsibility for your actions and decisions, even when things go wrong.

Assets – Things a person or business owns that have value, like cash, tools, or property.

Balance Sheet – A report that shows what a business owns (assets), owes (liabilities), and what's left for the owners (equity).

Break-Even Point – The moment when total income equals total costs — after that, the business starts making profit.

Budget – A plan for how to earn, save, and spend money wisely.

Cash Flow – The movement of money in and out of a business. Positive cash flow means more money coming in than going out.

Competitive Advantage – Something a business does better or differently than others, like higher quality, faster service, or a unique idea.

Compound Growth – Growth that builds on itself over time. For example, when you earn interest on both your money and the interest you already earned.

Cost Structure – The pattern of costs a business has, such as materials, labor, and rent.

Courage – Doing what's right even when it's difficult or unpopular.

Customer Happiness Score – A simple way to measure how pleased customers are with a product or service.

Decision-Making – Choosing among options after thinking about benefits, costs, and possible outcomes.

Efficiency – Doing a task in the best way possible with the least waste of time or resources.

Ethics – The values and rules that help people choose what's right, honest, and fair.

Fairness – Treating everyone equally and with respect; giving others what they deserve.

Forecasting – Using today's numbers to estimate what might happen in the future, such as next month's sales.

Honesty – Always telling the truth and admitting mistakes quickly.

Income Statement – A report that shows how much money a business earned, spent, and kept as profit during a certain period.

Integrity – Doing the right thing even when no one is watching; being true to your word and your values.

Internal Controls – Rules and checks inside a company that keep its money and records safe and accurate.

Inventory Turnover – How fast a business sells its products. A higher turnover means products are selling quickly.

Investment – Using money today to create more value or profit in the future.

KPI (Key Performance Indicator) – A special number that shows whether a business is reaching its goals, such as sales growth or customer satisfaction.

Liabilities – What a person or business owes, like loans or bills.

Long-Term Planning – Making decisions that prepare for success years into the future, not just for today.

Metrics – The specific numbers or measurements used to track progress and performance.

Opportunity Cost – The value of the next best thing you give up when making a choice.

Patience – Waiting calmly for results, knowing that long-term growth takes time.

Profit – The money a business keeps after paying all its costs.

Profit Margin – The percentage of money left as profit after all expenses are paid.

Reinvestment – Using some of a business's profits to buy better tools, train workers, or expand — to grow even more.

Resource Allocation – Deciding how to use limited things like money, time, or energy for the best results.

Revenue – The total amount of money earned from selling goods or services.

Risk Management – The process of identifying and reducing possible problems before they happen.

Scenario Planning – Thinking about "what-if" situations and preparing for different outcomes.

SEC (Securities and Exchange Commission) – A U.S. government agency that makes sure public companies tell the truth about their finances and follow fair rules.

Stakeholder – Anyone affected by a business's decisions, such as employees, customers, owners, or the community.

Strategic Planning – Setting long-term goals and deciding how to reach them step by step.

Sustainability – Running a business in a way that protects people, the planet, and profits for the future.

Transparency – Being open and clear about information so others can understand and trust you.

Trust – Confidence that others are honest and reliable.

Vision – A picture of what you want the future to look like — and the plan to make it happen.

Gross Profit – The money a business makes after subtracting only the cost of making or buying its products (like materials or supplies), but before paying other expenses such as rent or salaries.

Net Profit – The money left after subtracting **all** expenses — supplies, rent, pay, and taxes. This is the true profit a business keeps.

Ratio – A simple comparison between two numbers that helps show relationships, like how much profit is made from every dollar of sales. Ratios help Mini-CFOs spot patterns and make smart decisions.

CFO Strategy – The plan a Chief Financial Officer (CFO) uses to guide a business toward long-term success — balancing profit, growth, risk, and people. It's about seeing the big picture and making numbers work for the future.

✸ Epilogue —
Your Journey as a Mini-CFO

Professor FinanceWise stood before his students one last time beneath the tall Prosperity Tree. The golden leaves shimmered in the afternoon light, and the friends of Prosperity Hollow gathered around — Bella the Bunny, Max the Monkey, Timmy the Tortoise, and Lily the Ladybug — their notebooks full and their minds even fuller.

"Mini-CFOs," said the Professor, his voice calm and wise, "you've traveled far since the day you first asked, *What does a Chief Financial Officer do?*"

He looked around proudly.

"You've learned that money isn't just about coins and bills. It's about **choices, character, and courage.** You've learned to think ahead, balance risk, plan for growth, and build trust. That's what real financial leadership means."

What You've Learned on Your Journey

"Every great CFO once began with curiosity." — Professor FinanceWise

- **To Act and Learn:** You discovered that execution — taking the first small step — matters more than waiting for perfect plans.

- **To Save and Spend Wisely:** You practiced discipline, fixing the leaks and choosing what truly matters.

- **To Understand Business:** You looked behind the shop doors to see how profits, costs, and budgets shape success.

- **To Think Strategically:** You learned to use data, metrics, and strategy to build a lasting advantage.

- **To Lead with Integrity:** You discovered that honesty, fairness, and transparency are the invisible currencies that hold every business together.

Professor FinanceWise smiled.

"You've grown from a curious learner into a **Mini-CFO who can think, plan, and lead** — not just count money, but make it meaningful."

Your Mini-CFO Action Checklist

"Knowing is good. Doing is better." — Professor FinanceWise

Keep this checklist as your personal guide for real-world adventures:

1. **Plan Before You Spend** – Write down your goals before using your money.

2. **Save Something Every Time You Earn** – Even a small amount makes a big difference.

3. **Track Your Results** – Watch your savings and choices grow like a business dashboard.

4. **Ask Smart Questions** – Every great CFO keeps learning.

5. **Be Honest and Fair** – Integrity is your lifelong investment.

6. **Think Long-Term** – Build habits today that your future self will thank you for.

7. **Help Others Prosper** – True financial wisdom grows when shared.

🎓 **Print Your Mini-CFO Certificate (next page):**

⬛ **Certificate of Achievement**

This certifies that _____

has successfully completed the Mini-CFO Adventures journey and demonstrated

the qualities of curiosity, courage, character, and financial strategy.

Signed: _____

(Professor FinanceWise)

Date: _____

Professor FinanceWise congratulates you on completing your Mini-CFO journey!

www.ingramcontent.com/pod-product-compliance
Lightning Source LLC
Chambersburg PA
CBHW081816200326
41597CB00023B/4270